Biology
Experiments

Shortcuts to Success

Biology Experiments
for Leaving Certificate

Claire Daly

GILL & MACMILLAN

Gill & Macmillan Ltd
Hume Avenue
Park West
Dublin 12
with associated companies throughout the world
www.gillmacmillan.ie

© Claire Daly 2009
Artwork by Replika Press Pvt Ltd, India
978 0 7171 4431 0
Typeset by Replika Press Pvt Ltd, India

Contents

Note:

(a)   For experiments 8, 9 and 14, the student can choose to study *either* the enzyme amylase *or* catalase.

(b)   The student can choose to study experiment 19a *or* 19b.

TITLE 1a Conduct a qualitative test for starch

Aim

To test different solutions for the presence of starch. The chemical that will indicate if starch is present is iodine. Iodine turns from red-yellow to blue-black in the presence of starch.

Equipment and Materials

Balance • beaker (250 cm^3) • distilled water • dropper • iodine • labels • pipettes • soluble starch • spatula • test tube rack • test tubes • water bath • water bottle • waterproof pen • white tile.

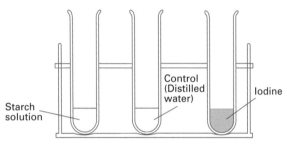

Safety Precautions

Before beginning this experiment, ensure that you have read the procedure thoroughly and have a clear understanding of how to perform the experiment in a safe manner.

Caution should be exercised when using the water bath, as steam and splashes from the boiling water can cause severe burns.

Iodine is harmful if swallowed, inhaled or if it comes in contact with the skin or eyes. A lab coat, disposable gloves and protective safety glasses should be worn while performing this experiment. Iodine should only be used in a well-ventilated area.

Toxic

Corrosive

Procedure

Prepare the Starch Solution (1%)

1. Prepare the starch solution (1%) by placing 1g of soluble starch into a beaker with 100 cm^3 of distilled water.
2. Place the beaker of starch solution into a water bath and set to 100°C.

3. When the solution has boiled, the starch should be fully dissolved and the solution should look clear. Allow the solution and water bath to cool.
4. If a lot of evaporation has occurred, more distilled water will need to be added to bring the solution back up to 100 cm^3.

Testing for Starch

1. Label three test tubes in the following manner and place in the test tube rack as shown in the diagram. Label one 'Iodine', label one 'Starch Solution' and label one 'Control' (this will contain distilled water).
2. Fill each of the test tubes with 2 cm^3 of their appropriate liquid. Use separate clean pipettes for each of the liquids.
3. Note the colours of the liquids in each of the test tubes. Hold a white tile behind each of the test tubes so that the colour can be seen more clearly.
4. Using the dropper, collect iodine from its test tube and place three drops in the test tube labelled 'Starch Solution' and three drops in the test tube labelled 'Control'. Do not insert the dropper into the liquids when dropping the iodine into the starch solution and the control.
5. Swirl each of the two test tubes to ensure that the iodine has mixed thoroughly with each of the liquids.
6. Observe the results of the experiment by noting the colour of the solutions in each test tube. Hold a white tile behind each of the test tubes so that the colour can be seen more clearly.
7. Record your results.

Results and Observations

On adding the iodine to the starch solution, the solution turned from a clear to a blue-black colour.

On adding the iodine to the control solution, the solution turned from a clear to a red-yellow colour.

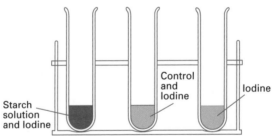

Colour of Solutions Before Iodine was Added	
A: Starch Solution	B: Control Solution
Clear	Clear
Colour of Solutions after Iodine was Added	
A: Starch Solution	B: Control Solution
Blue-Black	Red-Yellow

Control

The control in this experiment was the test tube with distilled water in it. Distilled water is very pure water and is not a source of starch.

Conclusions

The iodine turned from red-yellow to blue-black in the test tube labelled 'Starch Solution'. This shows that starch was present.

    The iodine remained red-yellow when added to the control in test tube 'Control Solution'. This shows that there was no starch present.

Possible Errors

A possible error that could occur in this experiment is that the experimenter may accidentally contaminate the solutions by touching the dropper off each solution as they are adding the iodine. This would be most problematic if the iodine is first added to the starch solution, as some of the starch solution may then be added to the control solution and a false positive may result.

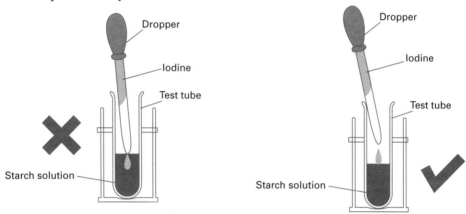

Application

See 'Application of Food Tests' on page 13.

Questions

1. List three foods that are a source of starch.
2. What was the name of the chemical that is used to test for starch?
3. What is the colour change that occurs with this chemical if placed in a starch solution?
4. Was heat required when testing the solutions for starch?
5. What was the control in this experiment?
6. What was the final colour of the control after the iodine was added to it? Explain why it was this colour.
7. Why was each test tube swirled after the iodine was added to it?
8. Give one safety precaution that should be observed when carrying out this experiment.
9. Give one possible source of error in this experiment.
10. What is the conclusion that can be drawn from this experiment?

TITLE 1b Conduct a qualitative test for a fat

Aim

To test different substances for the presence of a fat. When rubbed onto brown paper, fats leave a permanent translucent stain after drying.

Equipment and Materials

Brown paper • cotton buds • distilled water • droppers • labels • oil (olive, sunflower, vegetable) • test tube rack • test tubes • waterproof pen.

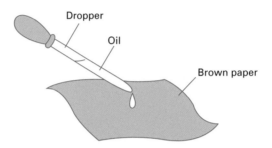

Safety Precautions

Before beginning this experiment, ensure that you have read the procedure thoroughly and have a clear understanding of how to perform the experiment in a safe manner.

Although this is not a dangerous experiment, fatty substances may stain clothes, so a lab coat should be worn.

Procedure

1. Label two test tubes, one as 'Oil' and the other as 'Distilled Water'. Fill both of the test tubes one-quarter full with their appropriate substance.
2. Take two pieces of brown paper and label one 'Oil' and the other 'Control'.
3. Using a clean dropper, add one or two drops of oil from its test tube to the piece of brown paper labelled 'Oil'. Rub the drops of oil onto the brown paper using a clean cotton bud.
4. Leave this brown paper to dry (near or on a radiator, on a windowsill or gently wave the paper through the air to initiate drying).
5. Using a clean dropper, add one or two drops of distilled water to the piece of brown paper labelled 'Control'. Rub the drops of distilled water onto the brown paper using a clean cotton bud.
6. Leave this brown paper to dry (near or on a radiator, on a windowsill or gently wave the paper through the air to initiate drying).
7. When dry, hold the two pieces of brown paper to a source of light and observe and compare them.
8. Record your results.

Results and Observations

On holding the dry piece of brown paper labelled 'Oil' to a light source, a permanent translucent stain can be seen on the paper.

On holding the dry piece of brown paper labelled 'Control' to a light source, no stain can be seen on the paper.

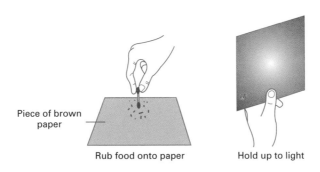

Piece of brown paper

Rub food onto paper   Hold up to light

Brown Paper	
Oil Added	**Distilled Water Added (Control)**
Permanent translucent stain on drying	No stain on drying

Control

The control in this experiment was the piece of brown paper with the distilled water added and rubbed onto it.

Conclusions

The oil must contain a fat, as it gave a positive result for fat, leaving a permanent translucent stain when rubbed onto brown paper. Oils are fats that are liquid at room temperature. The stain remained, as the fat does not evaporate from the brown paper. The distilled water was not a source of fat, as it did not leave a permanent translucent stain. The stain was not permanent, as the water evaporated from the brown paper.

Possible Errors

Cross-contamination could be a possible source of errors in this experiment. Points during the experiment where this is most likely to occur are when using the droppers and the cotton wool buds. When carrying out this experiment, if the same dropper was first used to collect some oil and then later to collect some water, the water may contain some oil that remained in the dropper and therefore the water would be contaminated and may lead to a false positive result. The same can be said of the cotton wool bud that is used to rub the oil onto the brown paper. If the same bud is first used to rub oil onto one piece of paper and then used later to rub distilled water onto the other piece of brown paper, oil that remained on the cotton wool bud may cause contamination and a false positive result.

Application

See 'Application of Food Tests' on page 13.

Questions

1. Other than types of oil, name two foods that are a source of fat.
2. What indicated a positive result in this experiment?
3. What safety precautions should be adhered to when carrying out this experiment?
4. Was heat essential for this experiment to occur?
5. What was the control for this experiment?
6. Explain why the oil left a permanent stain on the brown paper, yet the distilled water did not.
7. Give a possible source of error in this experiment.
8. Draw a diagram of the results that you obtained.
9. What conclusions can be drawn from this experiment?
10. Give an application for this experiment.

Aim

To test different solutions for the presence of a reducing sugar. The chemical that is used to test for a reducing sugar is Benedict's solution. When heat is applied, Benedict's solution turns from blue to brick red in the presence of a reducing sugar. The reducing sugars are the monosaccharides (glucose, fructose and galactose) and some of the disaccharides (lactose and maltose). Note that the disaccharide sucrose is not a reducing sugar.

Equipment and Materials

Balance • beaker (250 cm^3) • Benedict's solution • distilled water • droppers • labels • pipettes • reducing sugar (glucose) • spatula • test tube holders (or tongs) • test tube rack • test tubes • thermometer • water bath (electric or with Bunsen burner) • waterproof pen • white tile.

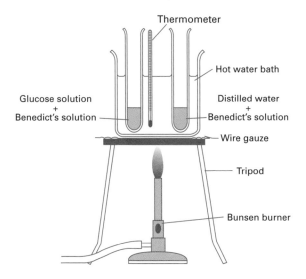

Safety Precautions

Before beginning this experiment, ensure that you have read the procedure thoroughly and have a clear understanding of how to perform the experiment in a safe manner.

Caution should be exercised when using the water bath, as steam and splashes from the hot water can cause severe burns. If using a Bunsen burner, be extremely cautious of the naked flame.

Benedict's solution is harmful if swallowed.

Harmful

Procedure

Prepare Glucose Solution (1%)

1. Prepare the glucose solution by dissolving 1g of glucose into some distilled water and then bring up to 100 cm^3 using water.

Testing for a Reducing Sugar

1. Turn on the water bath (or set a beaker of water on a tripod over a Bunsen flame and monitor the temperature of the water using a thermometer). Do not allow the water in the water bath to boil.
2. Label the three test tubes – one as 'Benedict's Solution', one as 'Glucose Solution' and one as 'Distilled Water' – and place them in the test tube rack.
3. Using a clean pipette each time, add 3 cm^3 of glucose and water to their appropriately labelled test tubes. In addition, add 7 cm^3 of Benedict's solution to its appropriate test tube.
4. Using a clean pipette, add 3 cm^3 of Benedict's solution to the test tube labelled 'Glucose Solution'.
5. Swirl the solution and note the colour of the glucose solution with the Benedict's solution added.
6. Using a clean pipette, add 3 cm^3 of Benedict's solution to the test tube labelled 'Distilled Water'. This will be the control of the experiment.
7. Swirl the solution and note the colour of the distilled water with the Benedict's solution added.
8. Place these two test tubes into the hot water bath. Leave the test tubes for five to ten minutes.
9. After the five to ten minutes have elapsed, use the test tube holders to lift each of the test tubes and observe their colours. Hold a white tile behind each of the test tubes so that the colour can be seen more clearly.
10. Record the colour of the solutions.
11. Turn off the water bath. Only remove the equipment that has been placed in the water bath after the water has cooled.

Results and Observations

On heating the glucose and Benedict's solution, it was noted that its colour had changed from blue to a brick red colour.

On heating the distilled water and Benedict's solution, it was noted that its colour had not changed from the blue colour.

	Before Heating	After Heating
Glucose Solution and Benedict's Solution	Blue	Brick Red
Distilled Water and Benedict's Solution	Blue	Blue

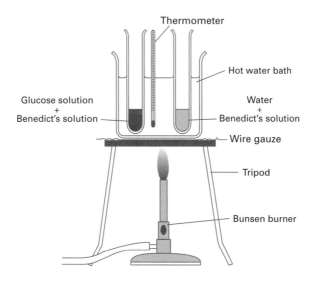

Control

The control in this experiment was the distilled water, as it does not contain any reducing sugars.

Conclusions

The glucose solution contained a reducing sugar as, when heated, the colour changed from blue to brick red.

The distilled water (control) did not contain a reducing sugar as, when heated, the colour remained blue.

Comments

Precautions should be followed when using a water bath, as the high temperatures could cause burns, e.g. do not handle the equipment in the water bath directly – use the test tube holders to lift the test tubes.

This experiment could also be carried out using Fehling's solution A and B instead of Benedict's solution. Equal volumes of Fehling's solution A and B are added together to give a blue solution. This solution is then used in place of Benedict's solution. The colour change for Fehling's solution indicating a positive result for reducing sugars is the same: when heat is applied, it changes from blue to brick red in the presence of reducing sugars.

Possible Errors

Possible cross-contamination could occur when adding the Benedict's solutions to the test tubes labelled 'Glucose Solution' and 'Distilled Water'. It is essential not to allow the dropper to touch the glucose solution or the distilled water when the Benedict's solution is added. If the dropper does touch the glucose solution when the Benedict's solution is added and is then used to transfer the Benedict's solution to the distilled water, cross-contamination will have occurred and this could lead to a false positive result. The most effective way to avoid this is to use separate clean droppers each time the Benedict's solution has to be added.

If the sample solution being tested does not have enough reducing sugars present, the colour may not reach a strong brick red colour. The sequences of colour changes that occur during this test are blue → green → yellow → red-orange → brick red.

Also, if you have not given your experiment enough time exposed to the heat, the full sequence of colours may not be completed to the brick red stage and your solution may, for example, appear more orange than brick red.

Application

See 'Application of Food Tests' on page 13.

Previous Exam Questions

2006 Higher Level

Q7 (a) (i)   State a use of each of the following in the biology laboratory.
      (ii) Benedict's (or Fehling's) test.
            To test for the presence of a reducing sugar.

Questions

1. Name three reducing sugars.
2. Name two food sources of reducing sugars.
3. Name the chemical that is used to test for the presence of reducing sugars.
4. What is a positive result for the presence of reducing sugars?
5. Is heat required in this experiment?
6. How was the temperature controlled in this experiment?
7. What is the control in this experiment and what is the result observed in the control?
8. Give one safety precaution that should be observed when carrying out this experiment.
9. Give a possible source of error in this experiment.
10. Explain what actions can be taken to reduce the possible error mentioned in the previous question.

Aim

To test different solutions for the presence of a protein. The chemicals that are used to test for this are sodium hydroxide, which is colourless, and dilute copper sulphate, which is blue. A positive result for the presence of a protein is when a combination of sodium hydroxide and dilute copper sulphate are added to a source of protein, their colour will go from blue to purple-violet.

Equipment and Materials

Dilute copper sulphate • distilled water • dropper • labels • pipettes • protein, e.g. albumin (egg white) • sodium hydroxide • test tube rack • test tubes • waterproof pen • white tile.

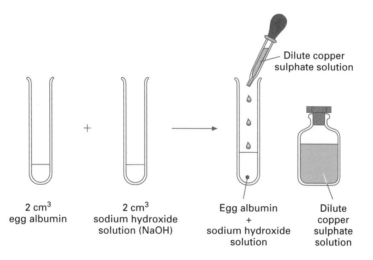

| 2 cm³ egg albumin | 2 cm³ sodium hydroxide solution (NaOH) | Egg albumin + sodium hydroxide solution | Dilute copper sulphate solution |

Safety Precautions

Before beginning this experiment, ensure that you have read the procedure thoroughly and have a clear understanding of how to perform the experiment in a safe manner.

Sodium hydroxide is very corrosive and can cause severe burns if it comes in contact with the skin or eyes. Damage to eyes may be permanent. It is also harmful if inhaled or ingested. When handling sodium hydroxide, always wear safety glasses and appropriate protective gloves.

Harmful

Corrosive

Dilute copper sulphate is harmful if swallowed or if its powder form is inhaled. It may cause irritation if it comes in contact with the skin or eyes. Safety glasses should be worn.

Harmful

Procedure

1. Label four test tubes with the following labels. Using clean pipettes each time, fill the test tube with the appropriate substance, then place in the test tube rack.
   (a) 'Albumin' (clear) – 2 cm^3
   (b) 'Distilled Water' (control, clear) – 2 cm^3
   (c) 'Sodium Hydroxide' (clear) – 5 cm^3
   (d) 'Dilute Copper Sulphate' (blue) – 2 cm^3
2. Using a clean pipette, place 2 cm^3 of sodium hydroxide into the test tube labelled 'Albumin' and place 2 cm^3 of sodium hydroxide into the test tube labelled 'Distilled Water'. Both the solutions will be clear upon adding the sodium hydroxide.
3. Using a clean dropper, place two to three drops of the dilute copper sulphate solution into the test tube labelled 'Albumin' and two to three drops of the dilute copper sulphate solution into the test tube labelled 'Distilled Water'. Upon adding the dilute copper sulphate solution, both the solutions will turn blue in colour.
4. Swirl each of the test tubes and observe any colour change. This can be seen more clearly by holding a white tile behind the test tube as you swirl the solution.
5. Record your results.

Results and Observations

On adding the sodium hydroxide and dilute copper sulphate to the albumin and swirling, this solution turned from blue to purple-violet.

On adding the sodium hydroxide and dilute copper sulphate to the distilled water and swirling, this solution remained blue.

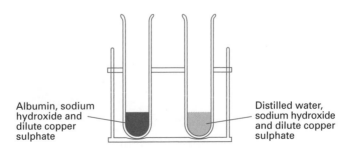

Albumin, sodium hydroxide and dilute copper sulphate

Distilled water, sodium hydroxide and dilute copper sulphate

	Immediate Colour	**Final Colour**
Albumin + Sodium Hydroxide + Dilute Copper Sulphate	Blue	Purple-Violet
Distilled Water + Sodium Hydroxide + Dilute Copper Sulphate	Blue	Blue

Control

The control in this experiment was the test tube containing the distilled water to which the sodium hydroxide and the dilute copper sulphate were added.

Conclusions

The conclusions that can be reached from these results are that the albumin solution contained protein, as the sodium hydroxide and dilute copper sulphate solution changed from blue to purple-violet in its presence.

The distilled water did not contain any protein as, when sodium hydroxide and dilute copper sulphate solutions were added to it, the solution remained blue.

Comments

This experiment could also be carried out by using Biuret reagent (2 cm^3) instead of the sodium hydroxide and dilute copper sulphate. The solution will be blue to begin with, but on contact with protein, it turns a purple-violet colour. Biuret reagent may cause irritation to the skin, eyes or respiratory system on contact. Safety glasses should be worn.

Possible Errors

If clean pipettes were not used when placing the appropriate substance in the test tubes at the beginning of the experiment, cross-contamination could occur and protein may then be found in the distilled water, therefore giving a false positive result.

Application of Food Tests

Many situations may arise where a scientist is faced with an unknown solution and is asked to investigate what it may be composed of (for example, a scientist working for a cleaning company or a forensic scientist may have to identify what caused a particular stain on clothes). Food tests would be simple tests that could be performed that can help to identify unknown substances.

Past Exam Questions

2007 Ordinary Level

Q8 (a) (i) State one reason why your body needs protein.
Your body needs protein for growth, maintenance and repair. Proteins also function as enzymes, antibodies or hormones. They may provide energy in cases where the body is suffering from starvation.

(ii) Name the element other than carbon, hydrogen and oxygen which is always found in protein.
Nitrogen.

(b)   Answer the following questions in relation to tests that you carried out for protein.

(i) Name two foods in which you found protein.
Albumin (egg white).
Meat.

(ii) What reagent or chemicals did you use to test for protein?
Sodium hydroxide and dilute copper sulphate.

(iii) Was heat necessary in the test that you carried out?
No.

(iv) What was the initial colour of the reagent or chemicals?
Blue.

(v) What colour change occurred if protein was present?
Purple-violet.

(vi) Was there a colour change in the control?
No.

2006 Higher Level

Q7 (a)   State a use of each of the following in the biology laboratory.

(i) Biuret test (copper sulphate and sodium hydroxide solutions).
To test for the presence of protein.

Questions

1. Name the two chemicals that are used to test for a protein.
2. Name a food source that contains protein.
3. What is the colour change that indicates a positive result for protein?
4. What was the control for this experiment?
5. What was the result for the control of this experiment?
6. Was heat required for this experiment?
7. Give two safety precautions that should be exercised when carrying out this experiment.
8. Give a possible source of error in this experiment.
9. Outline how the error that you mentioned in the previous question can be avoided.
10. What conclusions can be drawn from this experiment?

2 Identify any five fauna and any five flora using simple keys and identify a variety of habitats within the selected ecosystem

Aim

To be able to correctly identify any five different fauna (animals) and any five flora (plants) using simple keys to aid you. The fauna and flora can be identified from a selection of different habitats, e.g. grassland, seashore, woodland and hedgerow.

Equipment and Materials

Animal keys • binoculars • camera • clear plastic zip lock bags • jars • plant keys • samples of animals • samples of plants.

Simple animal key

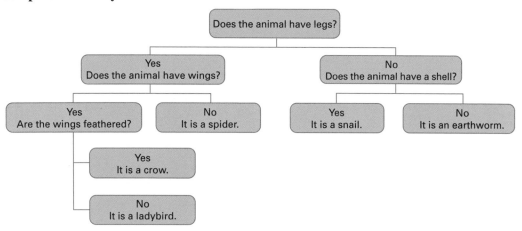

Simple plant key

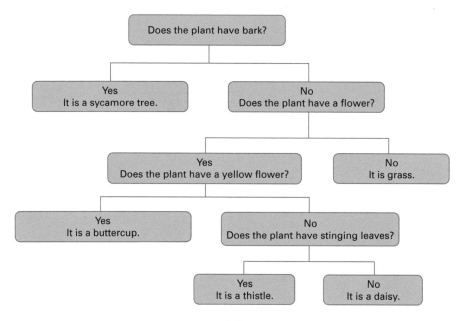

Safety Precautions

Before beginning this experiment, ensure that you have read the procedure thoroughly and have a clear understanding of how to perform the experiment in a safe manner.

When carrying out an ecological study in a habitat, ensure that you have asked the permission of landowners if entering private property. Always close gates after you so as not to accidentally release animals into areas where they should not be. Never approach any large animals, as they may charge, bite or kick. Be wary of small insects and certain plants, as they may cause stings. Extreme caution should be observed if working near large volumes of water.

Procedure

1. Draw a map of the habitat. Give a written description of the most important features of the habitat.
2. Use some of the collection methods mentioned in Experiment 3 to collect a selection of different organisms.
3. Note on your map of the habitat where all the organisms were observed or collected.
4. For larger organisms that may be difficult or dangerous to catch and collect, a photograph or a written description of the organism may have to suffice.
5. For any of the organisms that you may be unsure of or unable to identify, use the different keys available to make a positive identification.
6. When collecting samples of plants, do not take a large piece; instead, take a leaf and a flower (if present). Also take a photograph or write a description of any other unusual feature, e.g. does it have thorns? Is it climbing up a wall?
7. For any of the plants that you may be unsure of or unable to identify, use the different keys available to make a positive identification.
8. For all of the organisms found, note any adaptations that they may have to enable them to survive in their habitat.

Results and Observations

Fauna	
Ladybird *Adaptation:* Brightly coloured to indicate they are poisonous.	Spider *Adaptation:* Spins a web to enable it to catch its prey.
Earthworm *Adaptation:* Brown in colour ensuring they are camouflaged in the soil.	Snail *Adaptation:* Eyes on tentacles to increase field of vision.
Crow *Adaptation:* Strong beak to allow it to catch and eat its prey.	

Flora	
Grass  *Adaptation:* Green in colour for maximum photosynthesis.	Sycamore  *Adaptation:* Grows tall to ensure maximum exposure to light.
Buttercup  *Adaptation:* Produces flowers to attract insects of pollination.	
Daisy  *Adaptation:* Nectar is made to attract insects for pollination.	Thistle  *Adaptation:* Prickly leaves to avoid being eaten.

Control

There is no control for this experiment.

Conclusions

The conclusion that can be drawn from this experiment is that an identification key provides a very useful aid in correctly identifying an organism that you may previously not have recognised. These keys can be used to identify most plants and animals that can be found in your habitat.

Possible Errors

If the organism, especially animals, cannot be collected, any photographs, diagrams or descriptions of the organism may not provide all the information necessary to correctly identify the organism using an identification key.

Application

This can be useful in ecological research in identifying different plants and animals that may be present in the habitat, therefore providing fundamental information on the habitat.

2006 Higher Level

Q9 (a) (i)   What is meant by the term 'fauna'?
          The term 'fauna' relates to animals.

     (ii) In ecological studies, what is a key?
          In ecological studies, a key is used to help identify different types of plants and animals.

  (b) (i) Name five plants in the ecosystem that you have studied.
         1. Grass.
         2. Daisy.
         3. Buttercup.
         4. Thistle.
         5. Sycamore tree.

     (ii) In the space below, draw up a simple key which could be used to identify each of these plants.
          See 'Simple plant key' on page 15.

    (iii) Name five animals in the ecosystem that you have studied.
         1. Earthworm.
         2. Spider.
         3. Snail.
         4. Crow.
         5. Ladybird.

    (iv) In the space below, draw up a simple key which could be used to identify each of these animals.
          See 'Simple animal key' on page 15.

2004 Ordinary Level

Q8 (a) (i)   Name an ecosystem that you have studied.
          Grassland.

     (ii) Name three animals that are normally present in this ecosystem.
         1. Earthworm.
         2. Ladybird.
         3. Spider.

  (b) Select one of the animals that you have named in (a) and answer the following questions in relation to it.

     (i)   Which animal have you selected?
         Ladybird.

     (ii) State two features that allowed you to identify the animal.
         1. Ladybirds are brightly coloured with black spots.
         2. Ladybirds have six legs.

(iii) Name an organism on which this animal normally feeds.
Ladybirds normally eat aphids.

(iv) Explain how you attempted to find out how many of these animals were present in the ecosystem.
The capture recapture method is one way in which the numbers of ladybirds can be estimated in this habitat. A number of pitfall traps may be placed at random places in the habitat and the ladybirds that have been captured are marked and released. The pitfall trap is revisited the next day and the number of ladybirds is noted again. All the numbers of organisms are inserted into the capture recapture formula and the number of ladybirds in the habitat can be calculated.

(v) Using the axes below, draw a graph to show how you would expect the numbers of this animal to vary in the ecosystem in the course of a year.

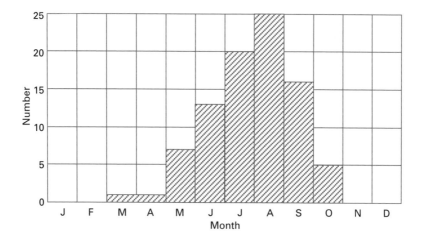

Questions

1. What is meant by the term 'fauna'?
2. What is meant by the term 'flora'?
3. Name five fauna that you identified on your field trip.
4. Name five flora that you identified on your field trip.
5. What aid does a key provide on an ecological field trip?
6. Give the identifying features for two fauna that you found while on your field trip.
7. Give the identifying features for two flora that you found while on your field trip.
8. Mention any distribution pattern that you noticed for one of the fauna you found while on your field trip.
9. Mention any distribution pattern that you noticed for one of the flora you found while on your field trip.
10. Give a safety precaution that you followed when carrying out this experiment.

3 Identify and use the various apparatus required for collection methods in an ecological study

Aim

In this experiment, a selection of different collection apparatus and methods will be employed to collect different organisms from the habitat. The correct use of the apparatus is essential if the organisms are to be collected, observed and recorded correctly.

Equipment and Materials

Beating tray • camera • cryptozoic trap • notepad • pitfall trap • plastic containers • pooter • secateurs • small mammal trap • soapy water • sweep net • Tullgren funnel • water net.

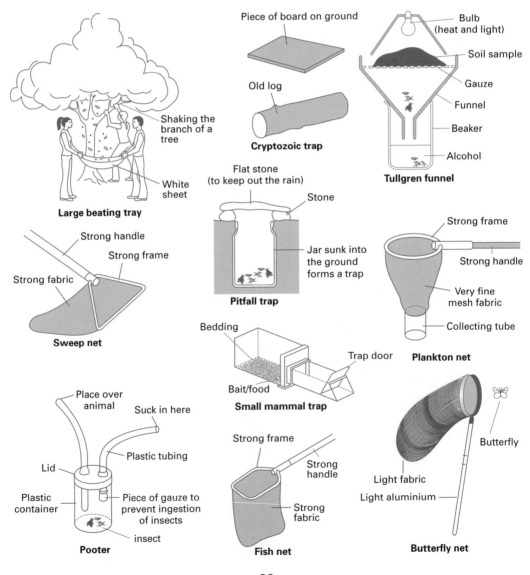

Large beating tray

Shaking the branch of a tree

White sheet

Piece of board on ground

Old log

Cryptozoic trap

Bulb (heat and light)

Soil sample

Gauze

Funnel

Beaker

Alcohol

Tullgren funnel

Strong handle

Strong frame

Strong fabric

Sweep net

Flat stone (to keep out the rain)

Stone

Jar sunk into the ground forms a trap

Pitfall trap

Strong frame

Strong handle

Very fine mesh fabric

Collecting tube

Plankton net

Bedding

Trap door

Bait/food

Small mammal trap

Place over animal

Suck in here

Lid

Plastic tubing

Plastic container

Piece of gauze to prevent ingestion of insects

insect

Pooter

Strong frame

Strong handle

Strong fabric

Fish net

Butterfly

Light fabric

Light aluminium

Butterfly net

Safety Precautions

Before beginning this experiment, ensure that you have read the procedure thoroughly and have a clear understanding of how to perform the experiment in a safe manner.

Caution should be exercised when choosing a place to position the collecting apparatus if they are to remain there for some time unattended, as people or animals could step into or onto them and cause damage to themselves or to the equipment.

When carrying out an ecological study in a habitat, ensure that you have asked the permission of landowners if entering private property. Always close gates after you so as not to accidentally release animals into areas where they should not be. Never approach any large animals, as they may charge, bite or kick. Be wary of small insects and certain plants, as they may cause stings. Extreme caution should be observed if working near large volumes of water.

Procedure

1. To collect samples of plant organisms, use a secateurs to remove some leaves and, if possible, flowers from the organisms.
2. Place these samples into individual rigid plastic containers and label them.
3. A written description, sketch or photograph of any other main features of this plant should also be recorded and kept with the plant sample to aid with later identification, if necessary.
4. To collect animals, a different approach is required. Take any of the following pieces of apparatus and use them appropriately to collect a number of organisms.
   (a) Name: Beating tray.
       How it is used: The beating tray is held under a bush or branch of a tree. The bush or branch is then shaken by hand or by using a large stick.
       Animals collected: Spiders, beetles, caterpillars, etc.
   (b) Name: Sweep net.
       How it is used: The sweep net is brushed through the vegetation as quickly as possible to increase the likelihood of catching insects. The lower rim of the net is flat, not rounded, so that it will have a greater surface area in contact with the ground.
       Animals collected: Spiders, beetles, caterpillars, butterflies, flies.
   (c) Name: Pooter.
       How it is used: The flexible straw is placed over the insect that is being observed. The student sucks through the rigid straw with the gauze on the bottom. This creates a vacuum which draws the insect into the jar. The purpose of the gauze is to prevent the organism from being sucked into the student's mouth.
       Animals collected: Spiders, beetles, flies, ants, woodlice, earwigs.
   (d) Name: Pitfall trap.
       How it is used: A small hole is dug in the ground and the jar of the pitfall trap is placed into the hole. The opening of the jar is covered over by a raised lid (a flat rock or a piece of wood). The covering is raised by small stones so that small organisms can crawl under the covering and fall into the jar. As the sides of the jar are steep and smooth, the insects cannot escape.

Animals collected: Spiders, slugs, snails, woodlice, earwigs, beetles, ants, centipedes, millipedes.

(e) Name: Small mammal trap.

How it is used: A small mammal trap is set up in the habitat with a food supply, a water supply and some bedding. It is important to provide these in the small mammal trap to allow the animal to be as comfortable as possible, as it will be in the trap overnight.

Animals collected: Field mice.

(f) Name: Cryptozoic trap.

How it is used: A cryptozoic trap can either be a flat piece of wood, a tile or a large, flat rock. These can be placed in several locations throughout the habitat and left there for a number of days or weeks. When they are ready to be studied, the cryptozoic trap can be lifted rapidly. All the organisms that have gathered underneath and are scrambling for shelter should be noted as quickly as possible. If possible, use a pooter to collect as many as the organisms as possible.

Animals collected: Spiders, slugs, snails, woodlice, earwigs, beetles, ants, centipedes, millipedes.

(g) Name: Tullgren funnel.

How it is used: A soil sample is placed in the Tullgren funnel and a bulb is lit very close to the soil sample. The bulb is covered above so all of its light and heat are directed onto the soil. This high light intensity and increase in temperature cause any of the organisms that are in the soil to move down deeper into the soil to escape them. The organisms that are moving down will pass through the gauze and fall into the alcohol or similar preserving fluid below.

Animals collected: Spiders, woodlice, earwigs, beetles, ants, centipedes, millipedes.

Results and Observations

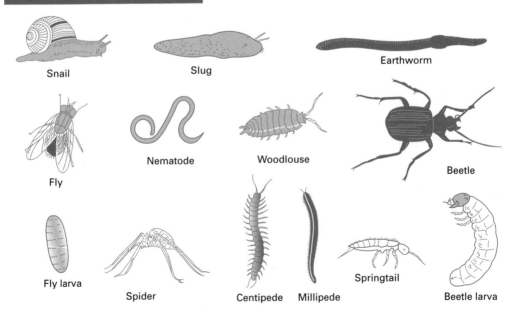

Snail

Slug

Earthworm

Fly

Nematode

Woodlouse

Beetle

Fly larva

Spider

Centipede   Millipede

Springtail

Beetle larva

Control

There is no control for this experiment.

Conclusions

This experiment shows that there is a wide variety of organisms present in a habitat. Although they may not always be visible, by using the most appropriate piece of equipment, many of them can be collected and their structures and life cycles can be studied in greater detail.

Possible Errors

With some of these methods of collection, the organisms may be aware of the movement of those setting the apparatus or collecting the insects; therefore, they may prove more difficult to catch.

Application

The collection of organisms is of great importance in ecological studies. Organisms need to be collected so that they can be identified, quantified in the habitat, researched and better understood.

Questions

1. Name three pieces of equipment that you used to collect the animals in your habitat study.
2. Describe how you collected plant samples.
3. Name an animal that was common to the habitat you studied and identify the piece of collection equipment that would be most suitable to collect it.
4. Draw a labelled diagram of two pieces of collection equipment.
5. What is the purpose of the gauze in a pooter?
6. What is the purpose of covering a pitfall trap with a raised flat rock?
7. Draw a labelled diagram of three types of animals you collected on your field trip.
8. Draw a labelled diagram of three plant samples that you collected on your field trip.
9. Give a safety precaution that should be followed when carrying out this experiment.
10. Give an application of collection methods in the field of ecology.

4 Conduct a quantitative study of plants and animals of a sample area of the selected ecosystem. Transfer results to tables, diagrams, graphs, histograms or any relevant mode

Aim

A quantitative study is one in which the number of a particular type of organism is researched using various methods. In this experiment, a quantitative study of some plant and animal populations will be carried out. The results will be presented in a suitable manner in diagrams, graphs, histograms or any other suitable method of presentation.

Equipment and Materials

Paper • pen • pitfall trap • quadrat with gridlines • small mammal trap • waterproof pen.

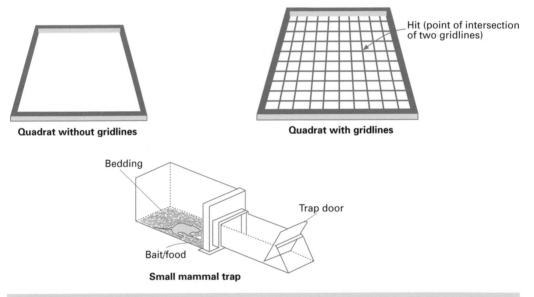

Quadrat without gridlines

Hit (point of intersection of two gridlines)

Quadrat with gridlines

Bedding

Trap door

Bait/food

Small mammal trap

Safety Precautions

Before beginning this experiment, ensure that you have read the procedure thoroughly and have a clear understanding of how to perform the experiment in a safe manner.

When carrying out an ecological study in a habitat, ensure that you have asked the permission of landowners if entering private property. Always close gates after you so as not to accidentally release animals into areas where they should not be. Never approach any large animals, as they may charge, bite or kick. Be wary of small insects and certain plants, as they may cause stings. Extreme caused should be observed if working near large volumes of water.

Care should be exercised when marking your captured animals. Ensure that you mark it in a way that does not change its chance of survival. The mark that you use should not cause injury or irritation, hinder the animal or make it more visible to its predators.

Always be cautious when placing the quadrat at random in the habitat. Never turn your back to the habitat and throw the quadrat randomly over your shoulder, as you may hit a person or an animal. Instead, work in groups so that one person can turn their back to the habitat and when the other group members indicate that it is safe, they can then throw a pen randomly over their shoulder. The quadrant is placed where the pen lands.

Procedure

Each of the following quantitative studies are best when carried out in groups in the habitat.

Calculating the Percentage Frequency

The percentage frequency method is used in the study of plants and slow-moving animals.

1. Working in groups, one member of the group stands with their back to the habitat with a pen in their hands. The other members of the group indicate when it is safe for the pen to be thrown at random into the habitat.
2. When the pen has been thrown, the members of the group that have a clear view of the habitat watch to see where the pen has landed. The quadrat is then placed where the pen has landed, with the pen in the centre.
3. The area of ground covered by the quadrat should be studied and all of the different organisms that are present should be listed and marked as being present in the first throw of the quadrat.
4. Steps 1, 2 and 3 should be repeated many times, e.g. fifty throws.
5. The percentage frequency of each organism in the habitat can now be calculated using the following formula:

$$\% \text{ Frequency} = \frac{\text{No. of quadrats containing organism}}{\text{No. of quadrats thrown}} \times 100$$

Calculating the Percentage Cover

The percentage cover method is used in the study of plants and slow-moving animals.

1. Working in groups, one member of the group stands with their back to the habitat with a pen in their hands. The other members of the group indicate when it is safe for the pen to be thrown at random into the habitat.
2. When the pen has been thrown, the members of the group that have a clear view of the habitat watch to see where the pen has landed. The quadrat (with gridlines) is then placed where the pen has landed, with the pen in the centre.
3. The area of ground covered by the quadrat should be studied and all of the different organisms that are present only at the cross-sections of the frame (hits) should be listed and marked as being present in the first throw of the quadrat.
4. Steps 1, 2 and 3 should be repeated many times, e.g. fifty throws.
5. The percentage cover of each organism in the habitat is calculated using the following formula:

$$\% \text{ Cover} = \frac{\text{No. of hits where organism was present}}{\text{Total no. of hits}} \times 100$$

Capture Recapture Method

The capture recapture method is used in the study of animal populations in a habitat. In this example, we will study the population of fieldmice.

1. Many small mammal traps are placed safely in different locations throughout the habitat. These traps should be left overnight and visited the next day.
2. Any fieldmice that are found in the traps should be marked in an appropriate way, recorded and then released back into the habitat.
3. When all the organisms have been marked, recorded and released, the traps are reset and left in a safe manner overnight.
4. The following day, the traps are revisited and the total number of fieldmice are recorded. The number of fieldmice that had previously been marked are also recorded.
5. The population of fieldmice in this habitat can then be calculated by using the following equation:

$$\text{Total Population} = \frac{\text{No. captured and marked on } 1^{st} \text{ visit} \times \text{No. captured on } 2^{nd} \text{ visit}}{\text{Number of marked animals on the } 2^{nd} \text{ visit}}$$

Results and Observations

$$\% \text{ Cover} = \frac{\text{No. of hits where organism was present}}{\text{Total no. of hits}} \times 100$$

Plant Name	Number of Times Present at a Hit per Throws of the Quadrat (25 Hits/Quadrat)										Total/250	% Cover
	1	2	3	4	5	6	7	8	9	10		
Grass	25	25	25	25	25	25	25	25	25	25	250	$\frac{250}{250} \times 100 = 100\%$
Clover	9	12	11	6	7	12	9	10	8	5	89	$\frac{89}{250} \times 100 = 36\%$
Buttercup	3	0	2	0	3	4	4	0	2	1	19	$\frac{19}{250} \times 100 = 8\%$
Daisy	0	3	7	0	2	1	4	3	5	2	27	$\frac{27}{250} \times 100 = 11\%$
Thistle	0	0	0	1	0	0	0	1	0	0	2	$\frac{2}{250} \times 100 = 1\%$

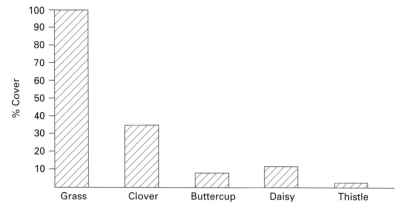

% Cover of plant found in habitat

	No. of quadrats containing organism
% Frequency =	$\dfrac{\text{No. of quadrats containing organism}}{\text{No. of quadrats thrown}} \times 100$

Plant name	\multicolumn{10}{c}{Number of Throws of Quadrat}	Total	% Frequency
	1	2	3	4	5	6	7	8	9	10		
Grass	✓	✓	✓	✓	✓	✓	✓	✓	✓	✓	10	$\frac{10}{10} \times \frac{100}{1} = 100\%$
Clover	✓	✓	✗	✓	✗	✓	✗	✓	✓	✗	6	$\frac{6}{10} \times \frac{100}{1} = 60\%$
Buttercup	✓	✗	✗	✓	✓	✗	✗	✗	✓	✓	5	$\frac{5}{10} \times \frac{100}{1} = 50\%$
Daisy	✗	✓	✗	✗	✗	✗	✓	✗	✓	✓	4	$\frac{4}{10} \times \frac{100}{1} = 40\%$
Thistle	✓	✗	✗	✗	✗	✗	✗	✗	✗	✗	1	$\frac{1}{10} \times \frac{100}{1} = 10\%$

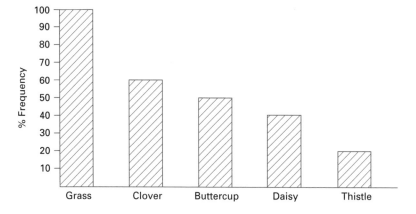

% Frequency of plants found in habitat

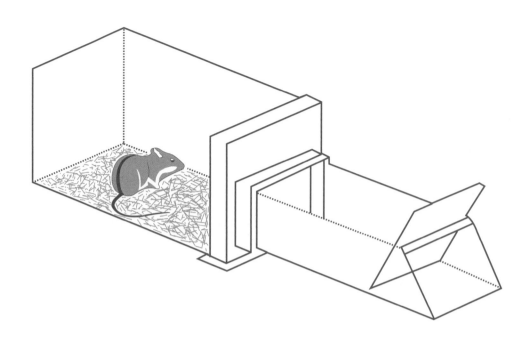

Capture Recapture Method (Population Size)			
No. of captured and marked on 1st visit $\times$ No. captured on 2nd visit No. of marked animals on the 2nd visit			
Animal Name	**No. of Organisms Caught on the 1st Day**	**No. of Organisms Caught on the 2nd Day**	**No. of Organisms Caught on Both Days**	**Population Size**
Fieldmouse	15	13	5	$\dfrac{15 \times 13}{5} = 39$

Control

There is no control for this experiment.

Conclusions

The conclusions for this experiment are the figures for the percentage cover and the percentage frequency of a number of plants that could be in that habitat and the population size of animals, e.g. fieldmice.

Comments

The results that were obtained for the percentage frequency, percentage cover and population size are only approximate figures for one particular day of the year. These figures will fluctuate on a seasonal, if not a daily, basis.

Possible Errors

A possible error that may be encountered in this experiment is a lack of random sampling as students may be tempted to continually position the quadrats on areas where there seems to be a good deal of variety in vegetation.

When performing the capture recapture method, errors that may arise are that the students may disturb the habitat so much or fail to add bait to the trap so that the animals may not approach the trap, that the animal is marked with something non-waterproof which washes away and cannot be seen upon recapture, and that the captured animals are not given enough time to disperse back into their habitat and are recaptured immediately upon release.

All of the above issues may lead to inaccurate figures regarding the species in your chosen habitat.

Application

The information that can be gained from this experiment would prove essential in any ecological study, providing information on the size of populations of the organisms in the habitat. This information would be vital in showing how the populations of these organisms fluctuate over time. These fluctuations in populations may then be researched and it may be found to be caused by changes in availability in food, increased numbers of predators or some other reason.

Past Exam Questions

2007 Ordinary Level

Q9 (a) (i) What is meant in ecology by a quantitative survey?
A quantitative survey is a survey where the number of organisms in an area is researched.

(ii) What is a quadrat frame?
A quadrat is a square frame that is used to sample a section(s) of a habitat in which all the species are noted and measured.

(b) Answer the following questions in relation to a quantitative survey of plants that you carried out.

(i) How did you use the quadrat frame to carry out the survey?
The quadrat was placed at random in the habitat and all of the species present were observed and measured.

(ii) Why did you use a number of quadrats or use the quadrat frame a number of times?
A number of quadrats were used to ensure a more accurate result and, therefore, a better representation of the habitat.

(iii) How did you identify the plants?
The plants were identified by using a plant key.

(iv) How did you present your results?
A table of all the results was drawn up. The results could also be presented in bar chart form using this information.

(v) Is the quadrat method suitable for animal populations? Explain your answer.
The answer for this will depend on the type of animal being studied. If the animal is very slow moving, e.g. a slug or snail, then, yes, it may be possible to use a quadrat. If the animal is fast moving, e.g. a fieldmouse, then, no, it may not be possible to use a quadrat.

2006 Ordinary Level

Q8 (a) (i) What is meant in ecology by a quantitative survey?
A quantitative survey is a survey where the number of organisms in an area is researched.

(ii) What is a quadrat frame?
A quadrat is a square frame that is used to sample a section(s) of a habitat in which all the species are noted and measured.

(b) (i) In the case of a named plant, describe how you would carry out a quantitative survey in the ecosystem that you have studied.
See the above procedure for this answer.

(ii) Describe how you recorded the results of your survey.
The results of the experiment were recorded in a table, as seen in the results sections above.

(iii) Suggest a possible source of error in your study.
A possible source of error in this study could be human error. For example, the number of organisms present in a quadrat may be incorrectly counted or the identification of a particular species may be difficult or may be incorrect. When the quadrat was being placed in the habitat, it may not have been done in a random way – students may have chosen areas which looked more interesting with a greater number and variety of plants present. This would result in an incorrect final result in the study.

Questions

1. What is the equation for percentage cover?
2. What information does the percentage cover give you about the population of a plant in a habitat?
3. What is the equation for percentage frequency?
4. What information does the percentage frequency give you about the population of a plant in a habitat?
5. What is the equation for the capture recapture method?
6. What information does the capture recapture method give you about the population of an animal in a habitat?
7. What is a quadrat frame?
8. Suggest how a quadrat frame can be used safely during a field trip.
9. How might a lack of randomness when using a quadrat affect the results of your experiment?
10. Give two recommendations for how to most effectively mark a captured animal without harming the animal.

5 Investigate any three abiotic factors present in the selected ecosystem. Relate results to choice of habitat selected by each organism identified in this study

Aim

In this experiment, three abiotic factors of the chosen habitat have to be investigated. The results of the investigations of each of these abiotic factors will then be used to show their impact on populations and locations of different organisms in the habitat.

Equipment and Materials

Air thermometer • compass • notepad • photographic light meter • waterproof pen • wind gauge.

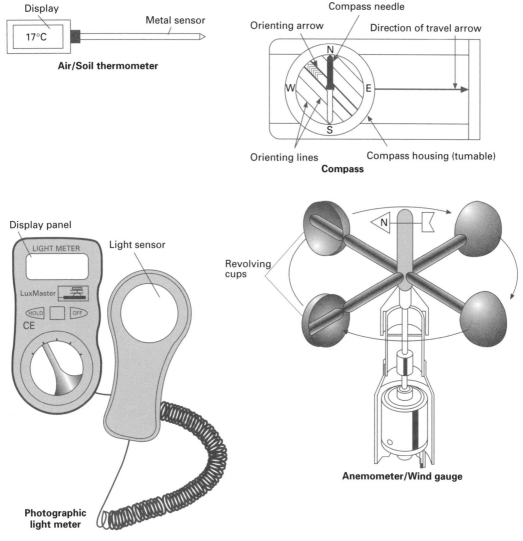

Display

17°C

Metal sensor

Air/Soil thermometer

Compass needle

Orienting arrow

Direction of travel arrow

N

W   E

S

Orienting lines

Compass housing (tumable)

Compass

Display panel

LIGHT METER

LuxMaster

HOLD   OFF

CE

Light sensor

Photographic light meter

N

Revolving cups

Anemometer/Wind gauge

Before beginning this experiment, ensure that you have read the procedure thoroughly and have a clear understanding of how to perform the experiment in a safe manner.

When carrying out an ecological study in a habitat, ensure that you have asked the permission of landowners if entering private property. Always close gates after you so as not to accidentally release animals into areas where they should not be. Never approach any large animals, as they may charge, bite or kick. Be wary of small insects and certain plants, as they may cause stings. Extreme caution should be observed if working near large volumes of water.

Procedure

1. Draw a map of the habitat and note the levels of three of the following abiotic factors at different locations around the habitat.

Aspect

1. The aspect of the habitat may be noted by using a compass to indicate the direction of north, south, east and west in the habitat.
2. These compass markings should be recorded and drawn onto the map.
3. When it is clear which are the north-facing and south-facing sides of the habitat, a comparative study of these sides of the habitat should be made.

Light Intensity

1. The light intensity of a habitat can be measured by using a photographic light meter.
2. When the photographic light meter is used, it is important that the cloud cover above the habitat is consistent each time a reading is taken. If the first reading is taken when there are blue skies above, the subsequent readings must also be taken when there are similar conditions.
3. Measurement of the light intensity is taken from different locations throughout the habitat.
4. The light intensity readings are recorded and the sites at which they are taken are noted and recorded onto the map. When several light intensity readings have been taken, a comparative study of areas with different light intensity should be carried out to see what influence light intensity has on the habitat.

Air Temperature

1. The air temperature can be taken using an air thermometer. Using the thermometer, take several air temperature measurements at different locations in the habitat.
2. Record the temperatures and indicate on the map where each temperature was taken.
3. When several air temperatures have been recorded, a comparative study of the areas with different temperatures should be carried out to see what influence air temperature has on the habitat.

Soil Temperature

1. Soil temperature can be measured using a thermometer. Using the thermometer, take several soil temperature measurements at different locations in the habitat.
2. Record the temperatures and indicate on the map where each temperature was taken.
3. When several soil temperatures have been recorded, a comparative study of the areas with different temperatures should be carried out to see what influence soil temperature has on the habitat.

Wind Gauge/Anemometer

1. The wind speed and direction can be measured using an anemometer. Using the anemometer, take several measurements of wind speed and direction at different locations in the habitat.
2. Record the measurements and indicate on the map where each of these measurements was taken.
3. When several measurements have been recorded, a comparative study of the areas with different wind speeds and directions should be carried out to see what influence wind speed and direction has on the habitat.

Results and Observations

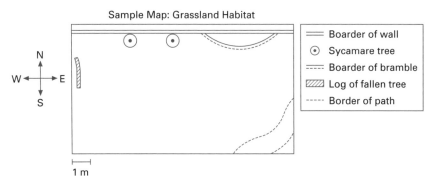

Sample Map: Grassland Habitat

=== Boarder of wall
⊙ Sycamare tree
----- Boarder of bramble
▧ Log of fallen tree
---- Border of path

1 m

Sample Results Early Spring. Conditions: Broken Cloud

- Wind Speed: 3 Beaufort Scale
- Wind Direction: South West
- Light intensity under tree: 600–750 × 100 Lux
- Light Intensity under tree: 210 × 100 Lux
- Light intensity in bramble area: 15 × 100 Lux
- Soil Temperature in open: 7–9°C
- Soil Temperatue in shade: 7.3°C
- Air Temperature in open: 8.4°C
- Air Temperature in shade: 7.2°C

Control

There is no control for this experiment.

Conclusions

Aspect: The south-facing side of the hedge will have a greater light intensity and therefore will have more vigorous growth.

Light intensity: The areas of the habitat that are exposed to the higher light intensities are more likely to have more vigorous growth of plants, the reason for this being that with the higher levels of light intensity, there will be higher levels of photosynthesis occurring and therefore an increased level of growth.

Wind speed and direction: The wind speed and direction will influence certain plants. For example, the growth of a tree will be greatest on the sheltered side.

Soil and air temperature: The soil and air temperatures are likely to be higher on the south-facing side of the habitat. Higher soil and air temperatures will result in more vigorous growth of plants in these areas, as the higher temperatures will be closer to the plant enzymes' optimum temperature of 25°C.

Comments

The results that we obtained for all of the above abiotic factors, with the exception of aspect, will fluctuate on a seasonal, daily and even momentary basis. Several visits at different times of the year would give the most accurate overall picture of how these abiotic factors affect the habitat.

Possible Errors

The most likely error to occur during this experiment is a failure of the students to use the instruments correctly. Even a student's shadow on the photographic light meter sensor can cause a false result to be recorded. Ensure that all students know how to use the equipment safely and accurately. Human errors in recording measurements can also occur so an effort should be made to double check these figures when they are being recorded. The worse the weather conditions, the more mistakes that are made in recording information.

Application

The information that is gained from this experiment would be of huge benefit to the agriculture and horticultural industries. By studying each of the abiotic factors and their influence on organisms, especially plants, in the habitat, a wealth of information can be gained. These results will mainly provide information about what the ideal growing conditions of each particular plant species are.

Questions

1. What is meant by 'abiotic factor'?
2. Name three abiotic factors that can influence the types of organisms that are found in a habitat.
3. Give an example of an abiotic factor that would primarily influence a terrestrial environment.
4. Give an example of an abiotic factor that would primarily influence an aquatic environment.
5. Name two abiotic factors and the equipment that you used to measure them.
6. Describe how one of the abiotic factors you mentioned influences a population of fauna that you studied on your field trip.

7. Describe how one of the abiotic factors you mentioned influences a population of flora that you studied on your field trip.
8. What is a possible error that may occur when carrying out this experiment?
9. Give an example of a safety precaution that should be followed when carrying out this experiment.
10. Give an application of this experiment in the field of ecology.

Aim

To be able to correctly use a light microscope to view a prepared slide under low and high power.

Equipment and Materials

Light microscope • prepared slides • soft cloth.

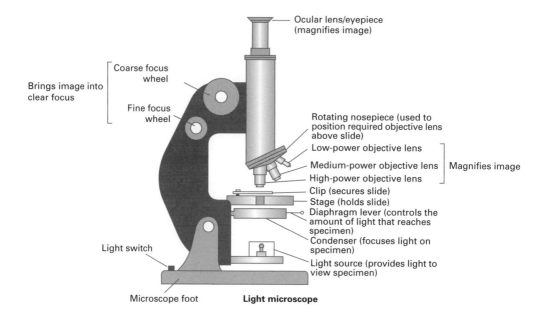

Ocular lens/eyepiece (magnifies image)

Coarse focus wheel

Brings image into clear focus

Fine focus wheel

Rotating nosepiece (used to position required objective lens above slide)

Low-power objective lens

Medium-power objective lens ⎤ Magnifies image

High-power objective lens

Clip (secures slide)

Stage (holds slide)

Diaphragm lever (controls the amount of light that reaches specimen)

Condenser (focuses light on specimen)

Light switch

Light source (provides light to view specimen)

Microscope foot **Light microscope**

Safety Precautions

Before beginning this experiment, ensure that you have read the procedure thoroughly and have a clear understanding of how to perform the experiment in a safe manner.

Caution should be exercised when bringing slides into focus, as the student may accidentally move the objective lens into the prepared slide, thereby breaking the slide and possibly the lens. This broken glass may cut the student.

Procedure

1. Before using the microscope, the student must identify each of the parts and functions labelled on the diagram of the microscope.
2. When ready to use the microscope, the eyepiece lens and the objectives lenses should be cleaned with a soft cloth to ensure that no dust or dirt is present that could obstruct the view of the slide.
3. Turn on or adjust the light source so that the light can be seen through the little hole on the stage.

4. Moving the nosepiece, place the lowest-power objective lens (the shortest of the objective lenses) into position for use. Move the objective lenses away from the stage. This may involve using either the stage height adjustment wheel or the coarse adjustment wheel, depending on the type of light microscope available.
5. Place the prepared slide on the stage and clip into place. Ensure that the cells of the slide are over the hole on the stage through which the light can be seen.
6. Before using the eyepiece to view the slide, place the low-power objective lens as close as possible over the slide without touching it.
7. Looking through the eyepiece, use the coarse adjustment wheel to bring the cells into focus by moving the objective lenses slowly upwards away from the slide. By focusing the cells in this way, you will not accidentally put the objective lens down and into the slide.
8. When the cells can be seen, sharpen the image by using the fine focus wheel.
9. When the cells are in focus, use the condenser, diaphragm or mirror (if present) to adjust the light so that the cells can be seen more clearly. If the sample is thin, this will often involve reducing the amount of light on the cells.
10. When the cells can be seen clearly, slowly move the slide on the stage so that the best section of the cells can be viewed.
11. Draw a diagram of the section of cells as seen under low power.
12. When the cells have been viewed under low power, use the nosepiece to move the next highest objective lens in position over the slide. When the next power objective lens is in position, the cells should already be in focus and the image may only need to be further sharpened by slowly using the fine focus wheel. The light may also need to be adjusted.
13. Draw a diagram of the section of cells as seen under high power.
14. When finished, turn the nosepiece so that the lowest-power objective lens is over the slide. Use the coarse adjustment wheel to move the stage to its farthest point away from the objective lens. Both these actions should provide enough room so that the slide can safely be removed from the microscope stage.

Results and Observations

The results for this experiment were that the student successfully used the microscope to view a slide. Below are some samples of tissues viewed using a light microscope.

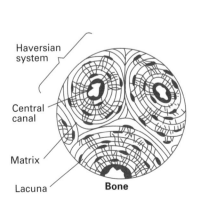

Haversian system · Central canal · Matrix · Lacuna · **Bone**

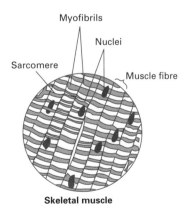

Myofibrils · Nuclei · Sarcomere · Muscle fibre · **Skeletal muscle**

There is no control for this experiment.

Conclusions

If the student was able to view the prepared slide through the microscope, the conclusion is that the student is familiar with and can use the light microscope.

Comments

Samples can only be viewed if they are translucent, as the light needs to be able to pass through the tissue sample to the lenses so that the tissue can be seen.

To calculate the total magnification being used to view the slide, use the following formula:

Magnification of eyepiece × Magnification of objective lens = Total magnification

Usually the eyepiece lens of a light microscope is ×10 and the objective lenses are ×4, ×10 and ×40.

Possible Errors

Possible errors in this experiment could include errors made when focusing or removing the slide that lead to damage of the slide or even the objective lens. If great care is not exercised, both the lens and the slide can easily be damaged.

Application

Microscopy (the use of microscopes) is of great importance in many areas of science. Microscopes are one of the main tools that are used in biological research (such as cytology, which is the study of the structure or function of cells) or as a diagnostic tool in biopsy (used to discover the presence or extent of a disease) or in autopsy (used to help determine the cause of death). Microscopes also play an important role in the study of evidence from crime scenes and help greatly the examination of the tiniest pieces of evidence.

Questions

1. What are the names of the two types of lenses on the light microscope?
2. What would be the total magnification being used if the eyepiece was ×10 and the objective lens was ×4?
3. What is the function of the nosepiece?
4. How many objective lenses are usually on a light microscope?
5. What is the function of the diaphragm?
6. What precautions should be taken when placing the slide on the stage so as not to damage the slide?
7. How is the slide secured onto the stage?
8. Why should the slide be brought into focus by moving the objective lens away from instead of towards the slide?
9. When using the low-power objective lens, what is the name given to the adjustment wheel that is used to bring the slide into focus?
10. Give an application of microscopes.

7a Prepare and examine one animal cell (unstained and stained) using a light microscope (×100, ×400)

Aim

To prepare two slides containing a sample of animal cells. One slide is to be left unstained, while the other slide is to have cells which have been stained. The recommended stain for this experiment is methylene blue. On preparation of the slides, both slides are to be viewed with the microscope under low power and high power. Diagrams of the two slides at low and high power are required as results.

Equipment and Materials

Cheek cells • cotton buds • cover slips • distilled water • droppers • glass microscope slides • labels • light microscope • methylene blue • seeker (for lowering the cover slip) • test tube rack • test tubes • timer • tissue paper • tray • wash bottle • waterproof pen.

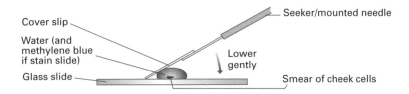

Safety Precautions

Before beginning this experiment, ensure that you have read the procedure thoroughly and have a clear understanding of how to perform the experiment in a safe manner.

Methylene blue is harmful if swallowed, inhaled or if it comes in contact with the skin. It also causes severe irritation to eyes. A lab coat, disposable gloves and protective safety glasses should be worn while performing this experiment.

Harmful

In this experiment, you are required to take a sample of your own cheek cells. One of the rules of being in a laboratory is that you do not place anything in or near your mouth, nose, ears or eyes. As we are required to place something in your mouth to collect the cheek cells, caution is required. Only use clean cotton buds to collect the cells from your mouth and when used, dispose of the cotton bud in the bin.

Procedure

1. Set up the microscope, ensuring that the light source is providing adequate light.
2. Label two test tubes, one as 'Methylene Blue' and one as 'Distilled Water'. Place these test tubes one-quarter full with their appropriate liquid into the test tube rack.
3. Label two slides on their ends, one as 'Stained' and the other as 'Unstained'. Place the two glass slides flat on some tissue on a tray to prevent staining the bench in case of spillages.
4. Using a clean cotton bud, rub the inside of your mouth to gather the cheek cells.
5. Smear the cotton bud with the cheek cells over a central section of the slide labelled 'Stained'.
6. Repeat step 4 and this time smear the cheek cells over the central section of the other glass slide labelled 'Unstained'.
7. Allow the cells to fix into position on the slide by letting them air dry for about one minute. When the cells are fixed in position, they are less likely to be washed away or damaged with the addition of water or stains.
8. Using a clean dropper, place one or two drops of methylene blue stain on the cheek cells that are smeared on the 'Stained' glass slide. Allow to soak for approximately one minute.
9. Using a clean dropper, place one drop of distilled water on each slide.
10. Using the seeker as an aid, place a cover slip over the sample of cells on both of the slides. The cover slip should be dropped slowly at an angle (45°) so that the air will be pushed out and will not be trapped under the cover slip, which could obscure your view of the cells.
11. If there is excess stain on the 'Stained' slide, the excess can be gently washed away using the wash bottle.
12. If there is excess liquid on the slides, gently soak up the excess by placing a clean corner of tissue or filter paper on the excess liquid.
13. Move the lenses of the microscope away from the stage. First place the 'Unstained' slide on the stage with the cell smear over the light source and secure into place using the clips.
14. Ensure that the low-power lens is over the sample. While looking at the microscope from the side, lower the lens as close as possible over the slide without touching the lens off the slide.
15. Looking through the eyepiece, bring the cells into focus by slowly moving the lens away from the slide. Note that as the cells on this slide are unstained, they will be difficult to see, great attention will be needed while focusing. When they come into focus, the unstained cells will look as if they were drawn with a faint leaded pencil. Carefully view the cells and ensure that you are able to differentiate between cells and debris, e.g. flecks of dust or fibres from the cotton buds.
16. When the cells can be seen, bring them into sharp focus by using the fine focus wheel.
17. Record your results by drawing what the cells look like at this magnification (×100).
18. When the cells have been observed and drawn at this magnification, use the nosepiece to place the next power lens over the slide. Do not adjust the height of the lens, because when the cells are in focus with the low-power objective lens, the

cells should still be in focus with the higher power objective lens and only minor adjustments to sharpen the image should be necessary.

19. Record your results by drawing what the cells look like at this magnification (×400). Note that no extra detail will be seen – the cells will just look bigger.
20. When you have made your drawings and are finished with the slide, move the lenses away from the stage and remove this slide.
21. The stain should be well absorbed into the cheek cells by now, so repeat steps 13 to 20 using the glass slide labelled 'Stained'.

Results and Observations

The cell ultrastructure that was visible using the light microscope was the cell membrane, the cytoplasm and the nucleus. These structures were visible in both the stained and unstained cells, but the addition of the methylene blue stain greatly improved the visibility of the structures, with the nucleus being most heavily stained, as the DNA absorbed the most stain.

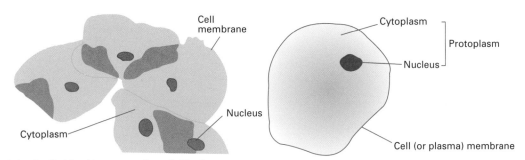

Animal cells (cheek) as seen using a light microscope   **ingle animal cell as seen using a light microscope**

Control

The unstained cells are the control in this experiment.

Conclusions

Light microscopes only have enough magnification to enable you to view some of the ultrastructures that are present in an animal cell.

Animal Cell Viewed with a Light Microscope	
Visible Ultrastructure	**Ultrastructure that is not Visible**
Cell Membrane	Mitochondria
Cytoplasm	Ribosomes
Nucleus	Nuclear pores
	Nucleolus

Comments

A clean spatula or a disposable inoculating loop may also be used to collect the cheek cells.

On completion of the experiment, all equipment that had contact with cheek cells should be disinfected if they are required for use again in another experiment (for example, the glass slides can be used again).

The addition of a cover slip onto a slide has many advantages. It keeps the cells of the sample from drying out, as the water and stain are trapped under the cover slip. It also protects the objective lens from dipping directly into the water and/or stain that may be present, therefore protecting both the lens and the sample from damage. The cover slip also helps to hold the sample of cells in position on the slide. Finally, the cover slip makes the sample of cells easier to view. By placing a cover slip over the sample of cells, less of the light is scattered from the curved surface of the drop of water. As a result of the cover slip's flat surface, more of the light makes it up from the slide into the objective lens; therefore, the object can be seen more clearly.

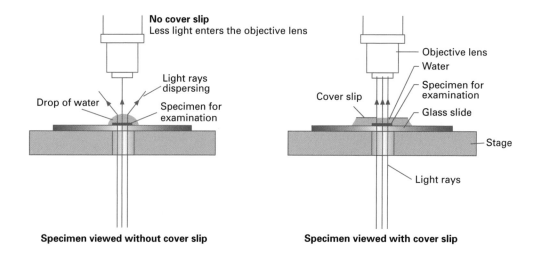

Specimen viewed without cover slip   Specimen viewed with cover slip

An alternative way of adding the stain to the sample of cells is as follows.

1. Fix the cells in position by letting them air dry for a minute.
2. Add a drop of water onto the sample of cells.
3. Add the cover slip at an angle.
4. Place a drop of the stain at one end of the cover slip and hold a piece of tissue paper or filter paper to the opposite side of the cover slip. The paper will draw liquid into it and therefore cause the stain to be drawn under the cover slip and over the cells.
5. When the stain is completely drawn over the cells and has reached the paper, remove the paper so no more liquid is soaked up.
6. Allow the stain to soak for one to two minutes.
7. Clean the slide of excess liquid using a clean piece of tissue before placing it on the stage of the microscope.

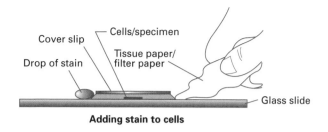

Adding stain to cells

Note that when you view the stained cells, the nucleus appears much darker (deep blue) than the cytoplasm (light blue). This is because the DNA absorbs more of the methylene blue stain than the cytoplasm.

Possible Errors

The cells may be brought into focus by moving the lens down towards the cells while viewing through the eyepiece. The problem with this method is that as you are looking through the eyepiece, you cannot see how close the lens is to the slide and if you miss the point where the cells are in focus (which can often happen if you are moving the lens too quickly or you blinked and missed them), you may end up pushing the lens through the cover slip of the slide. If this happens, you have ruined your slide and will have to prepare it again, but, more importantly, you may have ruined the lens. The correct way to focus on cells is while looking at the lenses from the side. Bring the lens down as close to the slide without touching it as possible and then bring the cells into focus by moving the lens away from the slide.

As with any experiment involving stains, be careful not to allow them to come in contact with your skin. Do not use excess stain and allow a few minutes for the stain to be absorbed into the cells for best results.

Application

Histology is the study of cells using a microscope. By knowing what healthy animal cells are supposed to look like, we can also identify abnormal cells. This is important in diagnosing different types of cancers by viewing cells taken in a biopsy. In a cervical smear test, cells of the cervix are removed and sent to a laboratory, where they are viewed under a microscope. If the cells appear abnormal, this may be the first indicator of cervical cancer. Also, during an autopsy, cells are taken and viewed and if abnormal may reveal the cause of death.

Past Exam Questions

2006 Higher Level

Q8 (a) State a function of each of the following components of a cell.

  (i) Ribosome
      The ribosome functions in protein synthesis.

  (ii) Cell membrane
       The cell membrane has many different functions. For example, it is a
       selectively permeable membrane and therefore controls what enters and

leaves the cell. It also contains the contents of the cell. In addition, it has receptors and can therefore recognise substances that touch it, e.g. hormones.

(b) Answer the following questions in relation to the preparation, staining and microscopic observation of a slide of an animal cell.

(i) What type of animal cell did you use?
Human cheek cells.

How did you obtain the cell?
The cells were obtained using a clean cotton bud and gently scraping the inside of the cheek (a clean spatula or disposable inoculating loop could also be used).

(ii) Name the stain that you used.
Methylene blue.

Describe how you applied the stain.
The stain was applied using a clean dropper to place a drop or two of the stain directly onto the cells. The stain was allowed to soak for approximately one minute.

(iii) After staining, a cover slip is placed on the slide. Give a reason for this.
There are a few beneficial reasons for placing a cover slip on the slide. Firstly, it can protect the objective lens from damage if it comes in direct contact with the slide. It protects the sample of cells from drying out by keeping the moisture trapped over the cells. It also helps to hold the cells in place. Finally, the cover slip makes it easier for the cells to be viewed, as more of the light is directed up into the lens by the cover slip.

(iv) How did you apply the cover slip?
The cover slip was applied by lowering it onto the sample of cells at an angle.

Why did you apply it in this way?
It was applied in this way to prevent air from becoming trapped under the cover slip. Air bubbles could obstruct the view of the cells.

(v) Describe the difference in colour or depth of colour, if any, between the nucleus and cytoplasm when the stained cell was viewed under the microscope.
The nucleus stained much darker than the cytoplasm, as the DNA absorbs more of the stain.

Questions

1. Briefly describe how the cheek cells were collected.
2. Why were the cells allowed to air dry on the glass slide?
3. What is the purpose of adding a stain to cells that are to be viewed using the microscope?
4. Name the stain that you used to stain the animal cells in this experiment.

5. On the stained slide, how does the nucleus appear in comparison to the cytoplasm?
6. Draw a labelled diagram showing how you placed the cover slip on the sample of cells.
7. Give two advantages of using a cover slip on a slide.
8. Name the structures of the animal cell that can be seen using the light microscope.
9. Give one safety precaution that should be exercised when carrying out this experiment.
10. Briefly describe how the slide should be correctly removed from the stage of the microscope.

Aim

To prepare two slides containing a sample of plant cells, e.g. onion cells. One slide is to be left unstained, while the other slide is to have cells which have been stained. The recommended stain for this experiment is iodine. On preparation of the slides, both slides are to be viewed with the microscope under low power and high power. Diagrams of the two slides at low and high power are required as results.

Equipment and Materials

Cover slips • distilled water • droppers • forceps • glass microscope slides • iodine • knife • labels • light microscope • onion • scalpel/scissors • seeker (for lowering the cover slip) • test tube rack • test tubes • timer • tissue paper • tray • waterproof pen.

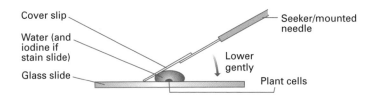

Safety Precautions

Before beginning this experiment, ensure that you have read the procedure thoroughly and have a clear understanding of how to perform the experiment in a safe manner.

Iodine is harmful if swallowed, inhaled or if it comes in contact with the skin or eyes. A lab coat, disposable gloves and protective safety glasses should be worn while performing this experiment. Iodine should only be used in a well-ventilated area.

Toxic

Corrosive

Caution should be exercised when using sharp blades. The cutting should always be done on a chopping board and the direction of the cutting should be away from the person's body.

1. Set up the microscope, ensuring that the light source is providing adequate light.
2. Label two test tubes, one as 'Iodine' and one as 'Distilled Water'. Place these test tubes one-quarter full with their appropriate liquid into the test tube rack.
3. Label two slides on their ends, one as 'Stained' and the other as 'Unstained'. Place the two glass slides flat on some tissue on a tray to prevent staining the bench in case of spillages.
4. Using the knife, cut the onion in half.
5. Use the forceps to lift a thin sheet of the onion tissue and cut with the scalpel/scissors.
6. With the help of a seeker, place the sheet of onion tissue flat on the central section of the slide labelled 'Unstained'.
7. Repeat step 5 and this time spread the onion cells over the central section of the other glass slide labelled 'Stained'.
8. Using a clean dropper, place one or two drops of iodine stain on the onion cells that are spread on the 'Stained' glass slide. Allow the stain to soak into the cells for approximately one minute.
9. Using a clean dropper, place one drop of distilled water on each slide.
10. Using the seeker as an aid, place a cover slip over the sample of cells on both of the slides. The cover slip should be dropped slowly at an angle (45°) so that the air will be pushed out and will not be trapped under the cover slip, which could obscure your view of the cells.
11. If there is excess liquid on the slides, gently soak up the excess by placing a clean corner of tissue or filter paper on the excess liquid.
12. Move the lenses of the microscope away from the stage. First place the 'Unstained' slide on the stage with the onion tissue over the light source and secure into place using the clips.
13. Ensure that the low-power lens is over the sample. While looking at the microscope from the side, lower the lens as close as possible over the slide without touching the lens off the slide.
14. Looking through the eyepiece, bring the cells into focus by slowly moving the lens away from the slide. Note that as the cells on this slide are unstained, they will be difficult to see, great attention will be needed while focusing. When they come into focus, the unstained cells will look as if they were drawn with a faint leaded pencil. Carefully view the cells and ensure that you are able to differentiate between cells and debris, e.g. flecks of dust or the dry, scaly outer layer of the onion.
15. When the cells can be seen, bring them into sharp focus by using the fine focus wheel.
16. Record your results by drawing what the cells look like at this magnification (×100).
17. When the cells have been observed and drawn at this magnification, use the nosepiece to place the next power lens over the slide. Do not adjust the height of the lens, as once the cells are in focus with the low-power lens, they should still be in focus with the higher power lens. Only minor adjustments to sharpen the image should be necessary.
18. Record your results by drawing what the cells look like at this magnification (×400). Note that no extra detail will be seen – the cells will just look bigger.

19. When you have made your drawings and are finished with the slide, move the lenses away from the stage and remove this slide.
20. The stain should be well absorbed into the onion cells by now, so repeat steps 12 to 19 using the glass slide labelled 'Stained'.

Results and Observations

The cell ultrastructure that was visible using the light microscope was the cell wall, cell membrane, the cytoplasm, large vacuole and the nucleus. These structures were visible in both the stained and unstained cells, but the addition of the iodine stain greatly improved the visibility of the structures, with the nucleus being most heavily stained, as the DNA absorbed the most stain.

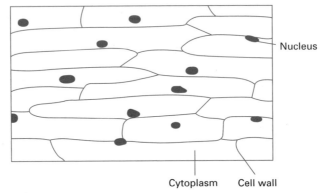

Plant cells (onion) as seen using a light microscope

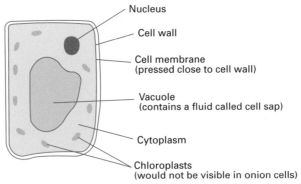

Single plant cell as seen using a light microscope

Control

The unstained cells are the control in this experiment.

Conclusions

Light microscopes only have enough magnification to enable you to view some of the ultrastructures that are present in the plant cell.

Plant Cell Viewed with a Light Microscope	
Visible Ultrastructure	**Ultrastructure that is not Visible**
Cell wall	Mitochondria
Cell membrane	Ribosomes
Cytoplasm	Nuclear pores
Vacuole	Nucleolus
Nucleus	
Chloroplast: In a sample of cells that were green in colour, these would be seen as tiny green specks throughout the cytoplasm of the cell. However, the onion cells are not green; therefore, we do not observe any chloroplasts.	

Comments

The addition of a cover slip onto a slide has many advantages. It keeps the cells of the sample from drying out, as the water and stain is trapped under the cover slip. It also protects the objective lens from dipping directly into the water and/or stain that may be present, therefore protecting both the lens and the sample from damage. The cover slip also helps to hold the sample of cells in position on the slide. Finally, the cover slip makes the sample of cells easier to view. By placing a cover slip over the sample of cells, less of the light is scattered from the curved surface of the drop of water. As a result of the cover slip's flat surface, more of the light makes it up from the slide into the objective lens; therefore, the object can be seen more clearly.

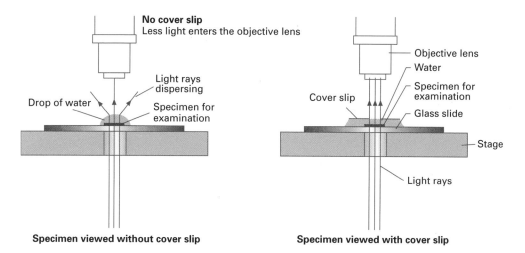

Specimen viewed without cover slip   Specimen viewed with cover slip

An alternative way of adding the stain to the sample of cells is as follows.

1. Fix the cells in position by letting them air dry for a minute.
2. Add a drop of water onto the sample of cells.
3. Add the cover slip at an angle.
4. Place a drop of the stain at one end of the cover slip and hold a piece of tissue paper or filter paper to the opposite side of the cover slip. The paper will draw liquid into it and therefore cause the stain to be drawn under the cover slip and over the cells.

5. Once the stain is completely drawn over the cells and has reached the paper, remove the paper so no more liquid is soaked up.
6. Allow the stain to soak for one to two minutes.
7. Clean the slide of excess liquid using a clean piece of tissue before placing it on the stage of the microscope.

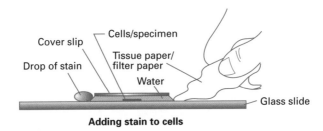

Adding stain to cells

Note that when you view the stained cells, the nucleus appears much darker (deep orange/brown) than the cytoplasm (light orange). This is because the DNA absorbs more of the iodine stain than the cytoplasm.

Possible Errors

The cells may be brought into focus by moving the lens down towards the cells while viewing through the eyepiece. The problem with this method is that as you are looking through the eyepiece, you cannot see how close the lens is to the slide and if you miss the point where the cells are in focus (which can often happen if you are moving the lens too quickly or you blinked and missed them), you may end up pushing the lens through the cover slip of the slide. If this happens, you have ruined your slide and will have to prepare it again, but, more importantly, you may have ruined the lens. The correct way to focus on cells is while looking at the lenses from the side. Bring the lens down as close to the slide without touching it as possible and then bring the cells into focus by moving the lens away from the slide.

As with any experiment involving stains, be careful not to allow them to come in contact with your skin. Do not use excess stain and allow a few minutes for the stain to be absorbed into the cells for best results.

Application

Histology is the study of cells using a microscope. Research into plant cells structures and functions are ongoing and the microscope plays an invaluable role in this. By knowing what healthy plant cells are supposed to look like under microscopes, we can also identify abnormal plant cells. This is important in diagnosing different types of plant diseases. Microscopes would also be required in the area of plant tissue culture.

Past Exam Questions

2004 Ordinary Level

Q7 (a)   Name the parts of the light microscope labelled A and B.

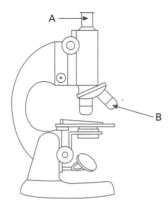

A = Eyepiece
B = Objective lens

If the magnification of A is ×10 and the magnification of B is ×40, what magnification results when a slide is viewed using B?
400.

(b) Answer the following in relation to preparing a slide of stained plant cells and viewing them under the microscope.

  (i) From what plant did you obtain the cells?
    An onion.

  (ii) Describe how you obtained a thin piece of a sample of the cells.
    The onion was first cut in half using a knife. Using a forceps, a thin layer of the onion cells was peeled away. A scalpel or scissors was then used to cut it away from the onion.

    What stain did you use for the cells on the slide?
    Iodine.

    Describe how you applied this stain.
    A dropper was used to place a drop of the iodine directly onto the onion tissue sample. An alternative method is to first add the water and cover slip onto the onion tissue. Then place a drop of the stain at one side of the cover slip and hold a piece of tissue paper or filter paper to the other side of the cover slip. The paper will draw the water over the cells, which in turn will cause the stain to be drawn over the cells.

    What did you do before placing the slide with the stained cells on the microscope platform?
    Before placing the slide on the microscope, the cover slip has to be correctly positioned on the slide by dropping it down at an angle. Also, any excess stain or water has to be cleaned from the surface of the slide using tissue or filter paper.

    State two features of these cells that indicate that they are typical plant cells.
    The presence of a cell wall and the presence of a large vacuole.

1. What is the name of the stain that is used to observe plant cells?
2. Briefly describe how the plant cells were removed from the plant to be placed on the slide.
3. What was the aim of this experiment?
4. What was the control in this experiment?
5. List the structures of a plant cell that are visible when viewed under a light microscope.
6. List the structures of a plant cell that are not visible when viewed under a light microscope.
7. List two structures of a plant cell you would not see in an animal cell when using a light microscope.
8. Give two safety precautions that need to be observed when performing this experiment.
9. Give an application of using the light microscope to view plant cells.
10. Draw a diagram of a plant cell as seen using a light microscope.

Aim

To discover the effect of pH on the rate of amylase activity. The experiment will be carried out three times, each time at a different pH (pH 4, 7 and 10). When carrying out the experiment at a certain pH, we will measure amylase activity by timing how quickly it was able to convert starch into maltose. We will measure this by using iodine in the experiment. Iodine turns blue-black in the presence of starch. A test for the presence of starch will be preformed at one-minute intervals. Eventually, as the enzyme has time to work, it may be recorded that all the starch has been digested to maltose. Therefore, when iodine is added, it no longer stains blue-black but remains a red-orange colour.

Equipment and Materials

Amylase • distilled water • droppers • electric balance • glass rods • iodine • labels • pH buffers 4, 7 and 10 • pH meter • pipettes • spatula • spotting tiles • starch solution • test tube rack • test tubes • thermometer • timer • tongs • water bath • waterproof pen • weigh boat.

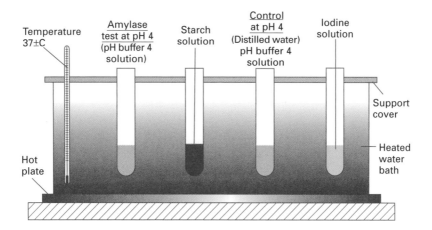

Safety Precautions

Before beginning this experiment, ensure that you have read the procedure thoroughly and have a clear understanding of how to perform the experiment in a safe manner.

Caution should be exercised when using the water bath, as steam and splashes from the hot water can cause severe burns. If using a Bunsen burner, be extremely cautious of the naked flame.

Iodine is harmful if swallowed, inhaled or if it comes in contact with the skin or eyes. A lab coat, disposable gloves and protective safety glasses should be worn while performing this experiment. Iodine should only be used in a well-ventilated area.

| Toxic | Corrosive |

Prepare the Starch Solution (2%)

1. Prepare the starch solution (2%) by placing 2g of soluble starch into a beaker with 100 cm^3 of distilled water.
2. Place the beaker of starch solution into a water bath and set to 100°C.
3. Once the solution has boiled, the starch should be fully dissolved and the solution should be clear. Allow the solution and water bath to cool.
4. If a lot of evaporation has occurred, more distilled water will need to be added to bring the solution back up to 100 cm^3.

Prepare the Amylase Solution (1%)

1. Prepare the amylase solution by placing 1g of soluble amylase powder into a beaker with 100 cm^3 of distilled water.

Investigate the Effect of pH on the Rate of Amylase Activity

1. Turn on the water bath and set it to 37°C.
2. Label two clean spotting tiles, one as 'Amylase Test at pH 4' and the other as 'Control at pH 4'.
3. Number each of the cavities in the spotting trays (1 to 15). Each cavity represents a one-minute interval.
4. Place these on the bench close to the water bath.
5. Label five test tubes with the following labels: 'Amylase', 'Starch', 'Iodine', 'pH Buffer 4' and 'Distilled Water'. Fill each test tube just over half full with its appropriate liquid.
6. Confirm the pH buffer strength using the pH meter.
7. Place all the test tubes in the water bath and allow them to come to 37°C. Confirm the temperature using the thermometer.
8. Label two clean test tubes, one as 'Amylase Test at pH 4'and another as 'Control at pH 4', and place them in the water bath.
9. Using a clean pipette, place 4 cm^3 of pH buffer 4 into both of these test tubes.
10. Place 2 cm^3 of amylase into the 'Amylase Test at pH 4' test tube.
11. Place 2 cm^3 of distilled water into the 'Control at pH 4' test tube.
12. Using a clean pipette, place 4 cm^3 of starch solution into both the 'Amylase Test at pH 4' and the 'Control at pH 4' test tubes.
13. On addition of starch to the solutions in the test tubes, immediately start the timer.
14. Using a clean glass rod each time, stir the contents of the 'Amylase Test at pH 4' and the 'Control at pH 4' test tubes.

15. Place a clean dropper in each of the two test tubes.
16. At one-minute intervals, using the assigned dropper, remove three to four drops of each liquid and place it in the appropriate cavity of the spotting tile.
17. Immediately add a drop of iodine to the drops of solution just placed in the spotting tray. Ensure that you use the clean dropper. Note and record the colours of the solutions.
18. Repeat steps 16 and 17 for fifteen minutes.
19. Repeat steps 5 to 18 using pH 7 and again using pH 10.

Results and Observations

The results that were observed from this experiment were as follows.

	Amylase Test Solution Results after 15 Minutes	(Distilled Water) Control Results after 15 Minutes
pH 4	Remained blue-black	Remained blue-black
pH 7	Was blue-black first then turned red-yellow after approximately 5 to 6 minutes	Remained blue-black
pH 10	Remained blue-black	Remained blue-black

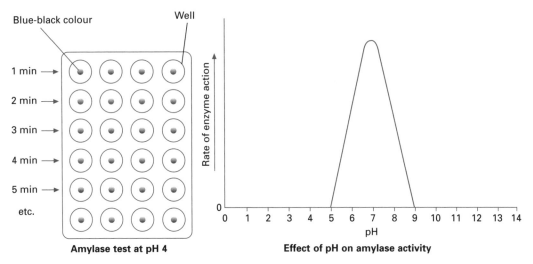

Amylase test at pH 4

Effect of pH on amylase activity

Control

The controls in this experiment were the test tubes at each pH that contained distilled water instead of amylase.

Conclusions

The pH of the solutions did have an effect on the rate of activity of amylase. As there was no activity of amylase at pH 4 and 10 after fifteen minutes, we can conclude that amylase must have been denatured at these pH levels, as they were too far outside the optimum range of this enzyme. At pH 7, the enzyme was shown to be active – it had the ability to convert the starch to maltose. Therefore, over time, the solution no longer stained blue-black when iodine was added; instead, it remained red-yellow. pH 7 has been shown to be this enzyme's optimum pH. None of the controls showed any activity. The conclusion that we can take from this is that amylase is needed to convert the starch to maltose.

Comments

The factors that were kept constant in this experiment were temperature, substrate concentration and enzyme concentration.

Temperature was kept constant by using a water bath. Substrate concentration was kept constant by making up a starch solution at the beginning of the experiment and adding the same volume of starch solution to the test tubes each time the experiment was carried out. Enzyme concentration was kept constant by making up an amylase solution at the beginning of the experiment and adding the same volume of amylase solution to the test tubes each time the experiment was carried out.

The factor that was varied in this experiment was the pH, which was varied by repeating the experiment using different pH buffers each time.

It is important to note that the rate of activity of an enzyme can also be affected by the freshness of the enzyme. As enzymes are protein, they are degraded and broken down over time, which could result in your amylase solution not having the concentration of enzyme you originally thought and therefore possibly not working as quickly as anticipated.

Possible Errors

If separate, clean pipettes and droppers were not used to transfer the different liquids into the different test tubes, cross-contamination could easily occur. For example, if the same dropper was first used to take up some starch solution and then used again to take up some distilled water, the distilled water could be contaminated with starch. Throughout this experiment, pipettes and droppers are used a great deal, so it is important that each pipette and dropper is only used to transfer one particular liquid. There is huge opportunity for cross-contamination if this is not adhered to.

Application

See 'Applications of Enzymes' on page 94.

Questions

1. Name amylase's substrate and product.
2. What was the control in this experiment?
3. How was the pH varied in this experiment?
4. What pH was shown to be amylase's optimum pH in this experiment?
5. Name a factor that was kept constant in this experiment.
6. How was the factor that you named in the previous answer kept constant in this experiment?
7. Give one safety precaution that should be exercised when performing this experiment.
8. Give one possible source of error in this experiment.
9. Briefly explain how the source of error you mentioned in the previous answer can be reduced.
10. What was the final conclusion that could be made from the results of this experiment?

Aim

To investigate if changing the pH of the enzyme catalase's environment will affect its ability to convert hydrogen peroxide to oxygen and water. This will be done by placing the enzyme and the substrate at a constant temperature of 25°C. A drop of washing-up liquid is added before the substrate is added. When the oxygen is released by the reaction, this oxygen will cause the washing-up liquid to froth. The activity of the enzyme can be related to the volume of the froth that is produced. The experiment is repeated at several different pH levels and the one in which the most froth is produced is the most suitable pH for this enzyme.

Equipment and Materials

Beakers • boiling tube • catalase, e.g. radishes • chopping board • distilled water • dropper • electronic balance • graduated cylinder • hydrogen peroxide • knife • labels • pH buffer 2, 6, 7, 9 and 11 • pH meter • spatula • test tube rack • thermometer • tongs • timer • washing-up liquid • water bath • waterproof pen • weigh boat.

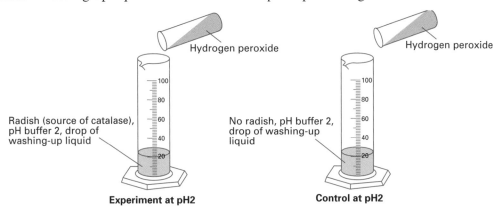

Radish (source of catalase), pH buffer 2, drop of washing-up liquid

Experiment at pH2

No radish, pH buffer 2, drop of washing-up liquid

Control at pH2

Safety Precautions

Before beginning this experiment, ensure that you have read the procedure thoroughly and have a clear understanding of how to perform the experiment in a safe manner.

Hydrogen peroxide is corrosive and can cause burns if it comes in contact with the skin or eyes. It is also harmful if inhaled or ingested. When handling hydrogen peroxide, always wear safety glasses and appropriate protective gloves.

Harmful

Corrosive

Procedure

1. Set a water bath to a temperature of 25°C.
2. Using the knife, finely chop the radish on the chopping board.
3. Label a graduated cylinder with 'Experiment at pH 2' and place in the water bath.
4. Label another graduated cylinder with 'Control at pH 2' and place in the water bath.
5. Label two boiling tubes as 'pH Buffer 2'. Using a clean pipette, place 15 cm^3 of pH buffer 2 into each of these boiling tubes.
6. Label a boiling tube as 'Washing-up Liquid'. Using a clean pipette, add a small amount (1–2 cm^3) of washing-up liquid to this boiling tube.
7. Label two boiling tubes as 'Hydrogen Peroxide'. Using a clean pipette, place 3 cm^3 of hydrogen peroxide into each of these boiling tubes.
8. Label a boiling tube as 'Radish Catalase'. Using an electronic balance and clean spatula, measure out and place 5g of finely chopped radish into this boiling tube.
9. Allow all of the items placed in the water bath to come to the correct temperature.
10. When they have reached the correct temperature, use the tongs to pour a test tube of pH buffer into each of the graduated cylinders.
11. Transfer the 5g finely chopped radish into the 'Experiment at pH 2' graduated cylinder.
12. Using a clean dropper, add one drop of washing-up liquid into each of the graduated cylinders.
13. Using the tongs, pour a test tube of the hydrogen peroxide into each of the graduated cylinders.
14. On addition of the hydrogen peroxide, immediately note the volumes of the liquid in the graduated cylinders and begin the timer.
15. After two minutes, observe and record the volume of the liquid in the graduated cylinder.
16. Repeat steps 2 to 15 at pH of 6, 7, 9 and 11.

Results and Observations

Catalase Test (25°C)					
pH of Buffer	2	6	7	9	11
Initial Volume (cm^3)	21	21	21	21	21
Final Volume (cm^3)	21	21	25.5	30	25
Volume of Foam Produced (cm^3)	0	0	4.5	9	4

Catalase Control (25°C)					
pH of Buffer	2	6	7	9	11
Initial Volume (cm^3)	18	18	18	18	18
Final Volume (cm^3)	18	18	18	18	18
Volume of Foam Produced (cm^3)	0	0	0	0	0

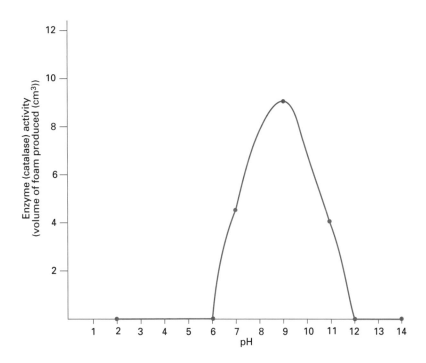

Control

The control for this experiment is to perform this experiment without the radish, and therefore without the enzyme catalase.

Conclusions

The conclusion that can be drawn from these results is that pH does affect the activity of the enzyme catalase. From these results, we can see that the optimum pH for the radish catalase is pH 9, as the greatest amount of foam was produced at this pH. There was no activity at pH levels of 2 and 6. Therefore, we can conclude that radish catalase is denatured at these pH levels. At the pH levels of 7 and 11, the enzyme showed activity, but it was not working at its optimum activity, as less foam was produced at these pHs. None of the controls showed any activity, which suggests that the enzyme catalase is essential, as the reaction could not take place without it.

Comments

The factors that were kept constant in this experiment were temperature, substrate concentration and enzyme concentration. Temperature was kept constant by using a water bath. Substrate concentration was kept constant by adding a set volume of hydrogen peroxide to the experiment each time the experiment was carried out. Enzyme concentration was kept constant by adding the same amount of finely chopped radish each time the experiment was carried out.

The factor that was varied in this experiment was the pH, which was varied by repeating the experiment using different pH buffers each time.

It is important to note that the rate of activity of an enzyme can also be affected by the freshness of the enzyme. As enzymes are protein, they are degraded and broken down over time, which could result in your catalase solution not having the concentration of enzyme you originally thought and therefore possibly not working as quickly as anticipated.

Possible Errors

If the volume of the fluid in the graduated cylinder is not measured immediately, the true volume of the foam produced may not be measured correctly and therefore an inaccurate final result may occur.

The amount of time that each experiment is given to produce foam must also be consistent so that the same parameters are applied to each experiment.

The washing-up liquid must be added to the enzyme before the substrate so that all of the product released can be measured. If it is added after the substrate, some of the oxygen will have already been released and the column of foam may not reach its full potential.

Application

See 'Application of Enzymes' on page 97.

Questions

1. What is the source of catalase in this experiment?
2. What is the name of the substrate of catalase?
3. Name a factor that is kept constant during this experiment.
4. How was this factor maintained at this constant level?
5. What is the function of the washing-up liquid in this experiment?
6. How was the activity of this enzyme measured?
7. What was the optimum pH of catalase?
8. Give a safety precaution that should be followed when doing this experiment.
9. What is the control of this experiment?
10. Give an application of enzymes in modern science.

9a **Investigate the effect of temperature on the rate of amylase activity**

Aim

To discover the effect of temperature on the rate of amylase activity. The experiment will be carried out a number of times, each time at a different temperature (0°C, 10°C, 20°C, 30°C, 35°C, 40°C, 45°C, 50°C and 60°C). When carrying out the experiment at a certain temperature, we will be able to measure the amylase's activity by timing how quickly it was able to convert starch into maltose. We will be able to measure this by using iodine in the experiment. Iodine turns blue-black in the presence of starch. At one-minute intervals, a test for the presence of starch will be preformed. Eventually, as the enzyme has time to work, it may be recorded that all the starch has been digested to maltose. Therefore, when iodine is added, it no longer stains blue-black but remains a red-orange colour.

Equipment and Materials

Amylase • distilled water • droppers • electronic balance • glass rods • iodine • labels • pH buffer 7 • pH meter • spatula • spotting tiles • starch solution • test tube rack • test tubes • thermometer • timer • water bath • waterproof pen • weigh boats.

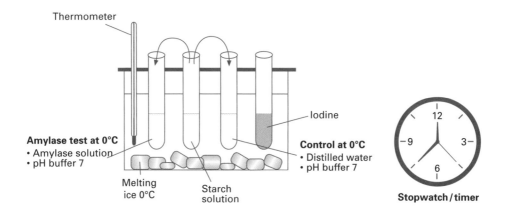

Safety Precautions

Before beginning this experiment, ensure that you have read the procedure thoroughly and have a clear understanding of how to perform the experiment in a safe manner.

Caution should be exercised when using the water bath, as steam and splashes from the hot water can cause severe burns. If using a Bunsen burner, be extremely cautious of the naked flame.

Iodine is harmful if swallowed, inhaled or if it comes in contact with the skin or eyes. A lab coat, disposable gloves and protective safety glasses should be worn while performing this experiment. Iodine should only be used in a well-ventilated area.

Toxic

Corrosive

Procedure

Prepare the Starch Solution (2%)

1. Prepare the starch solution (2%) by placing 2g of soluble starch into a beaker with 100 cm^3 of distilled water.
2. Place the beaker of starch solution into a water bath and set to 100°C.
3. When the solution has boiled, the starch should be fully dissolved and the solution should appear clear. Allow the solution and water bath to cool.
4. If a lot of evaporation has occurred, more distilled water will need to be added to bring the solution back up to 100 cm^3.

Prepare the Amylase Solution (1%)

1. Prepare the amylase solution by placing 1g of soluble amylase powder into a beaker with 100 cm^3 of distilled water.

Investigate the Effect of Temperature on the Rate of Amylase Activity

1. Set up a water bath at 0°C (use a beaker of iced water for the colder temperatures).
2. Label two clean spotting tiles, one as 'Amylase Test at 0°C' and the other as 'Control at 0°C'.
3. Number each of the cavities in the spotting tiles (1 to 15). Each cavity represents a one-minute interval.
4. Place these on the bench close to the water bath.
5. Label test tubes with each of the following labels: 'Amylase', 'Starch', 'Iodine', 'pH Buffer 7' and 'Distilled Water'. Fill each test tube just over half full with its appropriate liquid.
6. Place all of these test tubes in the water bath and allow them to come to 0°C. Confirm the temperature using the thermometer.
7. Label two clean test tubes, one as 'Amylase Test at 0°C' and another as 'Control at 0°C', and place in the water bath. Confirm the temperature using the thermometer.
8. Using a clean pipette, place 4 cm^3 of pH buffer 7 into both of these test tubes.
9. Place 2 cm^3 of amylase into the 'Amylase Test at 0°C' test tube.
10. Place 2 cm^3 of distilled water into the 'Control at 0°C' test tube.
11. Using a clean pipette, place 4 cm^3 of starch solution into both the 'Amylase at 0°C' and the 'Control at 0°C' test tubes.
12. On addition of starch to the solutions in the test tubes, immediately start the timer.
13. Using a clean glass rod each time, stir the contents of the 'Amylase Test at 0°C' and the 'Control at 0°C' test tubes.

14. Place a clean dropper in each of the two test tubes.
15. At one-minute intervals, using their assigned dropper, remove three to four drops of each liquid and place it in the appropriate cavity of the spotting tile.
16. After each minute, immediately add a drop of iodine to the drops of solution just placed in the spotting tray. Ensure that you use the clean dropper. Note and record the colours of the solutions.
17. Repeat steps 15 and 16 for fifteen minutes.
18. Repeat steps 5 to 17 at 10°C, 20°C, 30°C, 35°C, 40°C, 45°C, 50°C and 60°C.

Results and Observations

	Amylase Solution Time Taken for Colour to Change (Maximum Time Measured is 15 Minutes)	(Distilled Water) Control Time Taken for Colour to Change (Maximum Time Measured is 15 Minutes)
0°C	Colour remained blue-black	Colour remained blue-black
10°C	Colour remained blue-black	Colour remained blue-black
20°C	Colour remained blue-black	Colour remained blue-black
30°C	11 minutes	Colour remained blue-black
35°C	6 minutes	Colour remained blue-black
40°C	5 minutes	Colour remained blue-black
45°C	10 minutes	Colour remained blue-black
50°C	14 minutes	Colour remained blue-black
60°C	Colour remained blue-black	Colour remained blue-black

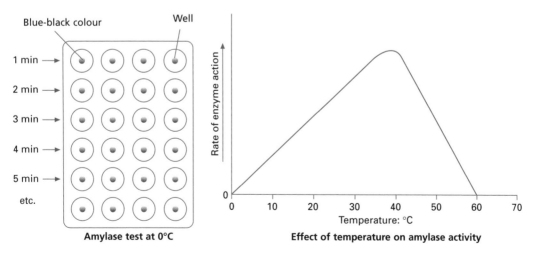

Amylase test at 0°C

Effect of temperature on amylase activity

Control

The controls for this experiment are the test tubes that contain distilled water instead of the enzyme amylase.

63

Conclusions

The conclusion for this experiment is that temperature did have an effect on the activity of the enzyme amylase as can be seen by the colour changes that were observed throughout the experiment. From these results we see that 40°C was the temperature at which the enzyme was most active.

The reason for this change in colour is that before the amylase was added to this test tube, the colour in the test tube was blue-black, as the iodine reacted with the starch. On addition of the amylase, this enzyme began to break down the starch to maltose. Therefore, the iodine was no longer able to react and the colour faded to red-orange.

Comments

The factors that were kept constant in this experiment were pH, substrate concentration and enzyme concentration. pH was kept constant by using a pH buffer. Substrate concentration was kept constant by making up a starch solution at the beginning of the experiment and adding the same volume of starch solution to the test tubes each time the experiment was carried out. Enzyme concentration was kept constant by making up an amylase solution at the beginning of the experiment and adding the same volume of amylase solution to the test tubes each time the experiment was carried out.

The factor that was varied in this experiment was the temperature, which was varied by repeating the experiment and setting the water bath to different temperatures and checking these temperatures with the thermometer. For the colder temperatures, an ice water bath was set up and its temperature monitored with the thermometer.

It is important to note that the rate of activity of an enzyme can also be affected by the freshness of the enzyme. As enzymes are protein, they are degraded and broken down over time, which could result in your amylase solution not having the concentration of enzyme you originally thought and therefore possibly not working as quickly as anticipated.

Possible Errors

If separate, clean pipettes and droppers were not used to transfer the different liquids into the different test tubes, cross-contamination could easily occur. For example, if the same dropper was first used to take up some starch solution and then used again to take up some distilled water, the distilled water could be contaminated with starch. Throughout this experiment, pipettes and droppers are used a great deal, so it is important that each pipette and dropper is only used to transfer one particular liquid. There is huge opportunity for cross-contamination if this is not adhered to.

Application

See 'Application of Enzymes' on page 94.

Past Exam Questions

2007 Higher Level

Q7 (a) (i) What is meant by an enzyme?
An enzyme is an organic catalyst made of protein that controls metabolic reactions.

(ii) Give an example of a protein that has a structural role.
Keratin is a protein which is found in hair, feather, hooves and horns. Actin and myosin are the proteins that make muscles. Collagen is an important protein found in skin, tendons and bones.

(b) Answer the following questions in relation to an investigation that you carried out to determine the effect of temperature on enzyme action.

(i) Name the enzyme that you used.
Amylase.

(ii) Name the substrate of the enzyme.
Starch.

(iii) State one factor that you kept constant during the investigation.
The pH, substrate concentration and enzyme concentration were kept constant during this investigation.

(iv) How did you keep this factor constant?
The pH was kept constant by using a pH buffer (a solution that can resist changes in pH and therefore keep the pH of a solution constant). The substrate concentration was kept constant by making up a starch solution at the beginning of the experiment and adding the same volume of starch solution to the test tubes each time the experiment was carried out. The enzyme concentration was kept constant by making up an amylase solution at the beginning of the experiment and adding the same volume of amylase solution to the test tubes each time the experiment was carried out.

(v) How did you vary the temperature?
The temperature was varied by setting the water bath to different temperatures and checking these temperatures with the thermometer. For the colder temperatures, an ice water bath was set up and its temperature monitored with the thermometer.

(vi) How did you measure the rate of activity of the enzyme?
The rate of activity of the enzyme was measured by timing how many minutes it took for all the starch (substrate) to be converted into maltose (product). This was done by removing some of the solution at one-minute intervals and testing for the presence of starch with iodine.

(vii) What was the result of your investigation?
The result of the investigation was that the different temperatures did have an effect on the rate of activity of amylase. The optimum temperature was seen to be 37°C. The more the temperature varied from this, the less active the enzyme was.

2007 Ordinary Level

Q7 (a) (i) Is an enzyme a lipid, a protein or a carbohydrate?
Protein.

(ii) Where in a cell are enzymes produced?
At the ribosomes.

(b) As part of your practical activities, you investigated the effect of temperature on the rate of activity of an enzyme.

(i) Name the enzyme you used.
Amylase.

(ii) Name the substrate with which the enzyme reacts.
Starch.

(iii) How did you vary the temperature?
The temperature was varied by setting the water bath to different temperatures and checking these temperatures with the thermometer. For the colder temperatures, an ice water bath was set up and its temperature monitored with the thermometer.

(iv) How did you keep a constant pH during the investigation?
The pH was kept constant by using a pH buffer (a solution which can resist changes in pH and therefore keep the pH of a solution constant).

(v) How did you measure the rate of activity of the enzyme?
The rate of activity of the enzyme was measured by timing how many minutes it took for all the starch (substrate) to be converted into maltose (product). This was done by removing some of the solution at one-minute intervals and testing for the presence of starch with iodine.

(vi) What was the result of your investigation?
The result of the investigation was that the different temperatures did have an effect on the rate of activity of amylase. The optimum temperature was seen to be 37°C. The more the temperature varied from this, the less active the enzyme was.

2005 Ordinary Level

Q8 (a) (i) What is an enzyme?
An enzyme is an organic catalyst made of protein that controls metabolic reactions.

(ii) Comment on the shape of enzyme molecules.
Enzymes are globular in shape. They are made up of long, folded chains of amino acids. Every enzyme has a portion called an active site whose shape matches that of a particular substrate. The active site can change shape slightly to fit more perfectly around its matching substrate when they are bound together.

(b) Answer the following questions in relation to an experiment that you carried out to investigate the effect of temperature on enzyme activity.

(i) What enzyme did you use?
Amylase.

(ii) What substrate did you use?
Starch.

(iii) Draw a labelled diagram of the apparatus that you used.
See the diagram on p. 61.

(iv) How did you know that the enzyme had completed its activity?
It was clear that the enzyme had completed its activity when the blue-black colour faded and the red-orange colour of iodine persisted. This showed that the enzyme had digested all the starch to maltose. Maltose does not react with iodine to produce a blue-black colour.

(v) How did you vary the temperature in your experiment?
The temperature was varied by setting the water bath to different temperatures and checking these temperatures with the thermometer. For the colder temperatures, an ice water bath was set up and its temperature monitored with the thermometer.

(vi) Draw an outline graph of the results that you obtained.

Questions

1. Clearly name the enzyme that you used in this experiment. Also name its substrate

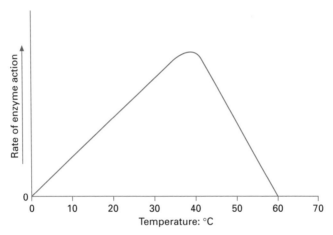

Effect of temperature on amylase activity

and product.
2. Name the factor that was varied in this experiment.
3. Explain how the factor mentioned in the previous question was varied.
4. Name two factors that were kept constant in this experiment.
5. Explain how the factors that were given in answer to the previous question were varied.
6. Give two safety precautions that should be followed when carrying out this experiment.
7. Outline a possible error that may occur in this experiment.
8. What were the results that were obtained from this experiment?
9. What conclusions can be drawn from this experiment?
10. Draw a graph showing the effect of temperature on the rate of activity of amylase.

TITLE 9b Investigate the effect of temperature on the rate of catalase activity

Aim

To investigate if changing the temperature of the catalase enzyme's environment will affect its ability to convert hydrogen peroxide to oxygen and water. This will be done by placing the enzyme and the substrate at a constant pH of 9. A drop of washing-up liquid is added before the substrate is added. When the oxygen is released by the reaction, it will cause the washing-up liquid to froth. The activity of the enzyme can to related to the volume of the froth that is produced. The experiment is repeated at several different temperatures and the one in which the most froth is produced is the most suitable temperature for this enzyme.

Equipment and Materials

Beakers • boiling tube • catalase, e.g. radishes • chopping board • distilled water • dropper • electronic balance • graduated cylinder • hydrogen peroxide • knife • labels • pH buffer 9 • pH meter • test tube rack • thermometer • tongs • timer • washing-up liquid • water bath • waterproof pen • weigh boat.

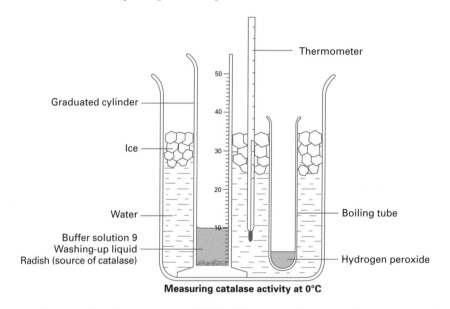

Measuring catalase activity at 0°C

Safety Precautions

Before beginning this experiment, ensure that you have read the procedure thoroughly and have a clear understanding of how to perform the experiment in a safe manner.

Caution should be exercised when using the water bath, as steam and splashes from the boiling water can cause severe burns.

Hydrogen peroxide is corrosive and can cause burns if it comes in contact with the skin or eyes. It is also harmful if inhaled or ingested. When handling hydrogen peroxide, always wear safety glasses and appropriate protective gloves.

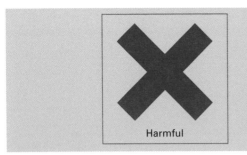
Harmful

Corrosive

Procedure

1. Use an ice water bath to achieve a temperature of 0°C.
2. Using the knife, finely chop the radish on the chopping board.
3. Label a graduated cylinder as 'Experiment' and place in the water bath.
4. Label another graduated cylinder as 'Control' and place in the water bath.
5. Label two boiling tubes as 'pH Buffer 9'. Using a clean pipette, place 15 cm^3 of pH buffer 9 into each of these boiling tubes.
6. Label a boiling tube as 'Washing-up Liquid'. Using a clean pipette, add a small amount (1–2 cm^3) of washing-up liquid to this boiling tube.
7. Label two boiling tubes as 'Hydrogen Peroxide'. Using a clean pipette, place 3 cm^3 of hydrogen peroxide into each of these boiling tubes.
8. Label a boiling tube as 'Radish Catalase'. Using an electronic balance and clean spatula, measure out and place 5g of finely chopped radish into this boiling tube.
9. Allow all of the items placed in the water bath to come to the correct temperature.
10. When they have reached the correct temperature, use the tongs to pour a test tube of pH buffer into each of the graduated cylinders.
11. Transfer the 5g of finely chopped radish into the 'Experiment' graduated cylinder.
12. Using a clean dropper, add one drop of washing-up liquid into each of the graduated cylinders.
13. Using the tongs, pour a boiling tube of the hydrogen peroxide into each of the graduated cylinders.
14. On addition of the hydrogen peroxide, immediately note the volumes of the liquid in the graduated cylinders and begin the timer.
15. After two minutes, observe and record the volume of the liquid in the graduated cylinder.
16. Repeat steps 2 to 15 at temperatures of 25°C, 55°C, 75°C and 100°C.

Results and Observations

Catalase Test (pH 9)					
Temperature (°C)	0	25	55	75	100
Initial Volume (cm^3)	21	21	21	21	21
Final Volume (cm^3)	21	25.5	30	26.5	21
Volume of Foam Produced (cm^3)	0	4.5	9	5.5	0

Control (pH 9)					
Temperature (°C)	0	25	55	75	100
Initial Volume (cm^3)	18	18	18	18	18
Final Volume (cm^3)	18	18	18	18	18
Volume of Foam Produced (cm^3)	0	0	0	0	0

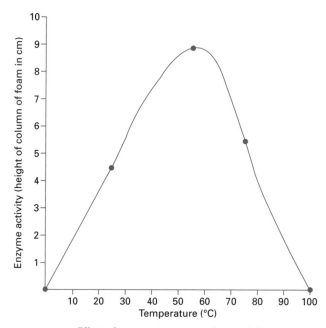

Effect of temperature on catalase activity

Control

The control for this experiment is to repeat this experiment using distilled water instead of the radish, and therefore without the enzyme catalase.

Conclusions

The conclusion that can be drawn from these results is that temperature does affect the activity of the enzyme catalase. From these results, we can see that the optimum temperature for radish catalase is 55°C, as the greatest amount of foam was produced at this temperature. There was no activity at temperatures of 0°C and 100°C. Therefore, we can conclude that radish catalase is denatured at these temperatures. At the temperatures of 25°C and 75°C, the enzyme showed activity, but was not working at its optimum activity, as less foam was produced at these temperatures. None of the controls showed any activity, which suggests that the enzyme catalase is essential. When it was not present, the reaction could not take place.

Comments

The factors that were kept constant in this experiment were pH, substrate concentration and enzyme concentration. pH was kept constant by using a pH buffer solution. Substrate concentration was kept constant by adding a set volume of hydrogen peroxide to the experiment each time the experiment was carried out. Enzyme concentration was kept constant by adding the same amount of finely chopped radish each time the experiment was carried out.

The factor that was varied in this experiment was the temperature which was varied by repeating the experiment using the water bath set at different temperatures.

It is important to note that the rate of activity of an enzyme can also be affected by the freshness of the enzyme. As enzymes are protein, they are degraded and broken down over time, which could result in your catalase solution not having the concentration of enzyme you originally thought and therefore possibly not working as quickly as anticipated.

Possible Errors

If the volume of the fluid in the graduated cylinder is not measured immediately, the true volume of the foam produced may not be measured correctly, therefore giving an inaccurate final result.

The amount of time that each experiment is given to produce foam must also be consistent so that the same parameters are applied to each experiment.

The washing-up liquid must be added to the enzyme before the substrate so that all of the product released can be measured. If it is added after the substrate, some of the oxygen will have already been released and the column of foam may not reach its full potential.

Application

See 'Application of Enzymes' on page 97.

Past Exam Questions

See the answers to the past exam questions for Experiment 9a on pp. 64–67, but note that some of the answers would need to be adjusted slightly to suit this experiment.

Questions

1. What is the source of catalase for this experiment?
2. What are the products of this enzyme?
3. What was the factor that was varied in this experiment?
4. How was this factor varied?
5. Give two safety precautions that should be followed when carrying out this experiment.
6. How was the pH of this experiment maintained at a constant level?
7. What was the purpose of the washing up liquid in this experiment?
8. What was the control of this experiment?
9. On addition of the substrate, what are the two important steps that need to take place?
10. Name two factors that are kept constant during this experiment.

TITLE 10 Prepare one enzyme immobilisation and examine its application

Aim

To immobilise an enzyme in a gel and then use this immobilised enzyme to produce a product. The enzyme that will be used in this experiment is sucrase. This enzyme is found in yeast, we will immobilise the yeast cells and thereby immobilise the enzyme. When using the immobilised enzyme in an application, we will place the immobilised enzyme in a sucrose solution and test for one of the products that should be made, namely glucose.

Equipment and Materials

Beakers (large) • calcium chloride • distilled water • electronic balance • glass rod • glucose test strips • labels • retort stands • separating funnels • sieve • sodium alginate • spatulas • sucrose solution • syringe • thermometers • wash bottles • water bath • waterproof pen • weigh boat • yeast.

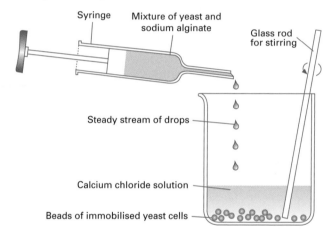

Preparing beads of immobilised yeast cells

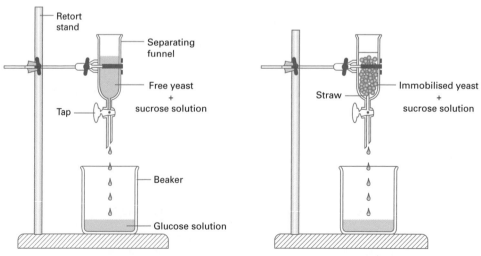

Comparing free yeast and immobilised yeast in making a product

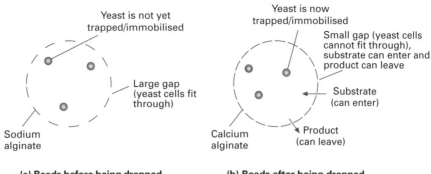

(a) Beads before being dropped in calcium chloride

(b) Beads after being dropped in calcium chloride

Safety Precautions

Before beginning this experiment, ensure that you have read the procedure thoroughly and have a clear understanding of how to perform the experiment in a safe manner.

Calcium chloride may cause irritation to the eyes and may be harmful if swallowed. Safety glasses should be worn.

Harmful

Procedure

Prepare the Immobilised Enzyme

1. Using a clean spatula and weigh boat each time, make up each of the following solutions.
2. Using a clean glass rod, thoroughly mix 0.8g of sodium alginate into 20 cm^3 of distilled water in a large beaker.
3. Using a clean glass rod, thoroughly mix 4g of dried brewer's yeast into 20 cm^3 of distilled water in a large beaker.
4. Pour 200 cm^3 of calcium chloride solution into a large beaker.
5. Pour the yeast solution into the sodium alginate solution and combine thoroughly with a clean glass rod.
6. Draw the yeast sodium alginate solution into a clean needle-less syringe.
7. Holding the syringe about 10 cm above the beaker containing the calcium chloride, slowly and steadily release the yeast and sodium alginate solution drop by drop into the beaker below.

8. Using a clean glass rod, gently stir the beads that form in the beaker of calcium chloride to prevent them from clumping together.
9. Continue to refill the syringe and form beads in the calcium chloride until you have an adequate number of beads.
10. When enough beads have been formed, allow them to harden for at least fifteen minutes.
11. When enough time has elapsed, pour the beads into a sieve and rinse with distilled water.
12. These beads can be stored immersed in distilled water for three to four days.

Application of the Immobilised Yeast Beads

1. Set up two separating funnels, each held over a large beaker.
2. Label one of the separating funnels as 'Immobilised Yeast' and one as 'Free Yeast'.
3. Make up a free yeast solution by using a clean glass rod to thoroughly mix 4g of dried brewer's yeast into 20 cm^3 of distilled water.
4. Pour this yeast solution into the appropriately labelled separating funnel.
5. Pour some of the beads into the appropriately labelled separating funnel.
6. Warm 100 cm^3 of water to 40°C in a water bath.
7. Make up a sucrose solution by mixing 1g of sucrose into the 100 cm^3 of warmed water.
8. Pour 50 cm^3 of the sucrose solution into each of the separating funnels.
9. Immediately release some liquid from the separating funnels and, using glucose test strips, test for the presence of glucose. Record your results.
10. Repeat this test for glucose at two-minute intervals until glucose is detected coming from each of the separating funnels. Record your results each time.
11. When the glucose has been detected coming from each of the separating funnels, all of the remaining solution can be released into the beakers below and the turbidity/cloudiness of the solutions can be compared and recorded.
12. Repeat this experiment without the yeast being present in the beads.

Results and Observations

The beads of immobilised enzymes were successful in their application of turning a substrate into a product.

Minutes Elapsed Before Glucose Was Detected				
	0	2	4	Turbidity
Free Yeast	A little glucose present	Glucose present	Glucose present	Cloudy
Immobilised Yeast	None	None	Glucose present	Clear

Control

The control for this experiment is to complete the experiment but without placing the enzymes into the beads.

Conclusions

The conclusion that can be drawn from this experiment is that by using immobilised enzymes, the product that is formed is much more pure than that made from free enzymes. The reason for this is that there are no enzymes mixed with the final product.

Possible Errors

It is very important that the yeast beads are rinsed with distilled water after they are first formed to ensure that there is no free yeast present on the outside of the yeast bead. If there is any free yeast on the outside of the beads, it could affect the results by causing glucose to appear as a product more quickly than it usually would. It would also affect the turbidity of the final product, as the free yeast may cause it to appear cloudy.

It is important to try to create a sterile environment in this experiment, as any micro-organisms that enter may become immobilised in the gel or may remain on the outside of the beads, which in turn may alter the experiment as previously described in the context of yeast.

Application

Immobilised enzymes are used a great deal in the field of biotechnology to make a wide range of different products, e.g. foods. When used in biotechnology, they provide a method by which a purer product can be made more cost effectively. This can be achieved because immobilised enzymes are more easily extracted from the final product, therefore making the end product more pure. Also, once extracted, the immobilised enzymes can be reused, therefore saving on costs. As the immobilisation process is a gentle one, the life of the enzyme is extended. As a result, less enzyme is required to be purchased, therefore helping to cut the costs of the industry.

Past Exam Questions

2005 Higher Level

Q7 (a)   Immobilised enzymes are sometimes used in bioreactors.

    (i)   What is a bioreactor?
A bioreactor is a container in which biological reactions can occur. They are used for many fermentation reactions in the biotechnology industry.

    (ii)   State one advantage of using an immobilised enzyme in a bioreactor.
The advantages of using an immobilised enzyme are that they are easier to remove from the product and the product will therefore be more pure. They are reusable, therefore they reduce costs. Immobilised enzymes have increased stability and therefore last longer than free enzymes.

(b)   Answer the following questions in relation to an experiment that you carried out to immobilise an enzyme and use that immobilised enzyme.

    (i)   Name the enzyme that you used.
Sucrase is the enzyme that was used. It is found in yeast.

(ii) Draw a labelled diagram of the apparatus that you used to immobilise the enzyme.
See the diagram on p. 72.

(iii) Describe how you used this apparatus to immobilise the enzyme. In your answer, name the solutions that you used and explain their purpose.
See the 'Prepare the Immobilised Enzyme' procedure on page 73.

(iv) Describe briefly how you used the immobilised enzyme.
The immobilised enzyme was used to digest sucrose into glucose and fructose.

Questions

1. What is the name of the enzyme that is immobilised in this experiment?
2. What is the substrate and what is the product of this enzyme?
3. What is the name of the organism that contains the enzyme?
4. What are the two chemicals that are used to immobilise the enzyme?
5. What techniques can be used to help form the beads with the immobilised enzymes?
6. Why are the beads of the immobilised enzymes rinsed after they are formed?
7. Give a safety precaution that should be observed while carrying out this experiment.
8. Suggest a possible error that may occur during this experiment and how it may be avoided.
9. Give an application of immobilised enzymes.
10. Give a benefit of immobilised enzymes.

11 Investigate the influence of light intensity on the rate of photosynthesis

Aim

The rate of photosynthesis in plants can be influenced by a number of things, such as temperature, carbon dioxide concentration and light intensity. In this experiment, we will keep all conditions constant except light intensity. By doing this, we can measure the effect that changing the light intensity has on the rate of the plant's photosynthesis. An aquatic plant is used in this experiment, as the oxygen produced in photosynthesis can be seen moving up through the water. The rate of photosynthesis can be more easily measured by counting the average number of bubbles of oxygen that are released from the plant per minute at each level of light intensity.

Equipment and Materials

Aquatic plant, e.g. elodea • backed blade • beaker • boiling tube • chopping board • forceps • lamp • light meter (optional) • measuring tape/metre stick • pH buffer 7 • pond water • sodium bicarbonate • spatula • timer • thermometer • weight, e.g. paper clip.

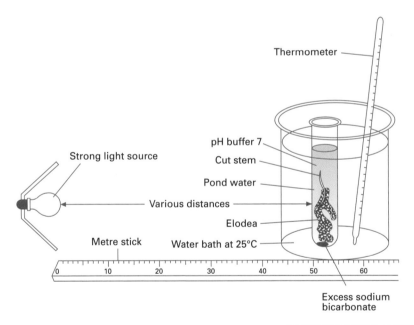

Safety Precautions

Before beginning this experiment, ensure that you have read the procedure thoroughly and have a clear understanding of how to perform the experiment in a safe manner.

Caution should be exercised when using sharp blades. The cutting should always be done on a chopping board and the direction of the cutting should be away from the person's body.

Procedure

1. Fill a boiling tube with distilled water.
2. Place the boiling tube in a water bath at 25°C. Use a clean spatula to add excess of sodium bicarbonate to the boiling tube.
3. Using a clean pipette, add 1–2 cm^3 of pH buffer 7 to the boiling tube.
4. Use the backed blade to cut the stem of the elodea at an angle. Also remove any leaves that are present near the end of the stem.
5. If the elodea floats in the water, attach a weight to keep it at the bottom of the boiling tube.
6. Place the apparatus in a darkened area.
7. Place the lamp 1 m away from the apparatus and switch it on.
8. Allow the elodea five minutes to adjust to and reach its maximum rate of photosynthesis at this light intensity.
9. Start the timer and count the bubbles of oxygen that are leaving the elodea in one minute. Record the results. Repeat this for a total of three minutes and then calculate and record the average number of bubbles released from the stem of the elodea per minute.
10. Move the lamp to a distance of 80 cm, 60 cm, 40 cm and 20 cm away from the apparatus and repeat steps 8 and 9 at each of these distances.

Results and Observations

Distance from Light Source (cm)	Light Intensity $(1/d^2)$	Count 1 (Bubbles/Min)	Count 2 (Bubbles/Min)	Count 3 (Bubbles/Min)	Average
20	2.5×10^{-3}	20	22	21	21
40	6.25×10^{-4}	10	11	12	11
60	2.77×10^{-4}	5	3	4	4
80	1.56×10^{-4}	1	0	1	0.67

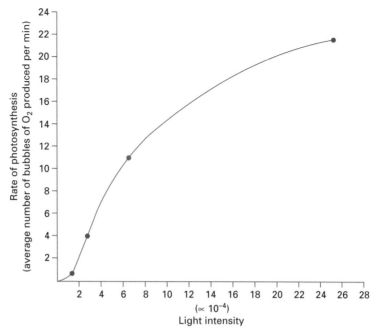

Effect of light intensity on the rate of photosynthesis

There is no control for this experiment.

Conclusions

As the light intensity increases, so too does the number of bubbles of oxygen produced per minute. However, the number of bubbles would only increase up to a certain point, after which the elodea is then said to be light saturated. This means that no matter how much light the elodea is exposed to, it is unable to photosynthesise any faster.

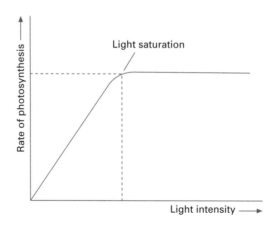

Comments

When preparing the elodea, the stem had to be cut at an angle, as this enables the oxygen to escape from the stem more easily. A number of the closest leaves to the cut stem were also removed so as not to obscure the view of the oxygen leaving the cut end of the stem.

The pH of this experiment was maintained at 7 and the temperature was maintained at 25°C, as these are suitable conditions for photosynthesis in elodea.

Excess sodium bicarbonate was added to the water surrounding the elodea in this experiment. The sodium bicarbonate releases carbon dioxide into the water. By having excess carbon dioxide present, we are ensuring that carbon dioxide does not become a limiting factor which could influence the results of the experiment.

Possible Errors

The error that is most likely to occur in this experiment is that each time the light intensity is altered, the plant is not given enough time to adjust. Therefore the counting of the O_2 bubbles leaving the plant begins too early, leading to inaccurate results.

Application

Knowledge of how to increase the rate of photosynthesis would be of great importance to horticulturalists and agriculturalists. If the factors that affect the rate of photosynthesis are understood, an environment can be adjusted so that the plants have the optimum conditions for photosynthesis to occur. These optimum conditions are usually provided in a greenhouse. The benefit of a plant carrying out photosynthesis at its maximum rate is that it will be producing a great deal of glucose, which in turn will result in a general increase in the plant's size and an increase in the plant's yield or size of flowers, fruit or vegetables.

Past Exam Questions

2007 Higher Level

Q9 (a) State a precise role for each of the following in photosynthesis:

   (i) Carbon dioxide
        Supplies the carbon necessary for the production of glucose.

   (ii) Water
        Supplies the hydrogen that is used in the production of glucose, and electrons that give energy to aid in the production of glucose.

   (b) Answer the following questions in relation to an activity that you carried out to investigate the influence of light intensity or carbon dioxide concentration on the rate of photosynthesis.

   (i) Name the plant that you used.
        Elodea.

   (ii) How did you vary light intensity or carbon dioxide concentration?
        The light was varied by placing a lamp at different distances from the plant.

   (iii) State a factor that you kept constant during the investigation.
        CO_2 concentration, temperature and pH were kept constant during this investigation.

(iv) How did you ensure that the factor that you mentioned in (iii) remained constant?

CO$_2$ was kept constant by adding excess sodium bicarbonate to the water in which the plant was placed. The temperature was kept constant by using a water bath. The pH was kept constant by using a pH buffer solution.

(v) How did you measure the rate of photosynthesis?

The rate of photosynthesis, at each light intensity, was measured by counting the average number of bubbles of O$_2$ that were released from the cut stem of elodea per minute.

(vi) Using labelled axes, sketch a graph to show how the rate of photosynthesis varied with the factor mentioned in (ii) above.
See the diagram on page 79.

Questions

1. Why was an aquatic plant used for this experiment?
2. How was the elodea prepared for this experiment?
3. What is the factor that is varied in this experiment?
4. How was the above factor varied?
5. What was the function of the sodium bicarbonate?
6. Name three factors that were kept constant in this experiment.
7. For all of these factors, mention how they were kept constant.
8. How was the rate of photosynthesis measured?
9. What is the name given to the point at which the rate of photosynthesis does not increase even if the light intensity does?
10. Suggest a possible error that may occur in this experiment and how it may be avoided.

Aim

When yeast respire anaerobically, they convert glucose into alcohol and carbon dioxide. In this experiment, the yeast will be placed in anaerobic conditions and alcohol and carbon dioxide will be produced. The presence of carbon dioxide can be measured by limewater and the alcohol can be measured by performing the idoform test.

Equipment and Materials

Boiling tube • concentrated sulphuric acid • conical flask • distilled water • dropper • fermentation locks • filter paper • glass tubing • glucose solution • limewater • oil • pH buffer 7 • potassium iodide solution • sodium hypochlorite • water bath • yeast.

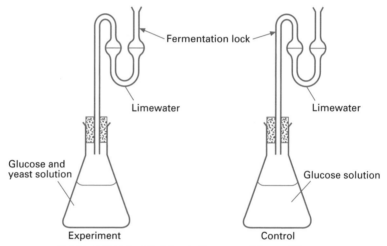

Equipment and materials creating anaerobic conditions

Safety Precautions

Before beginning this experiment, ensure that you have read the procedure thoroughly and have a clear understanding of how to perform the experiment in a safe manner.

Caution should be exercised when using the water bath, as steam and splashes from the boiling water can cause severe burns.

Potassium iodide may cause irritation to the skin, eyes or respiratory system on contact. Safety glasses and appropriate protective gloves should be worn.

Harmful

Corrosive

Sodium hypochlorite is corrosive and can therefore cause burns if it comes in contact with the skin or eyes. It is also harmful if inhaled or ingested and produces a poisonous gas if combined with an acid. Safety glasses and appropriate protective gloves should be worn. Sodium hypochlorite should only be used in a well-ventilated area.

Harmful

Corrosive

Ethanol is highly flammable and therefore needs to be used away from sources of heat and in a well-ventilated area. Irritation is caused if it comes in contact with the eyes, so safety glasses must be worn.

Highly Flammable

Harmful

Procedure

1. Make up a 10% glucose solution by dissolving 60g of glucose into 600 ml of distilled water.
2. Pour 300 ml of this glucose solution into a conical flask.
3. Place the conical flask with the glucose solution into a boiling water bath for five minutes to help remove a lot of the oxygen from the solution, therefore making a more anaerobic solution.
4. Allow the glucose solution to cool and then add 7g of yeast to the solution. If the yeast is added to the hot glucose solution, the enzymes in the yeast will become denatured due to the high temperature.
5. Half fill a fermentation lock with limewater.
6. Place this fermentation lock onto the conical flask.
7. On careful inspection, bubbles of CO_2 may be seen exiting the surface of the yeast and glucose solution.
8. For the control, repeat the experiment with the remaining glucose solution, but this time without the yeast included.
9. Place both of these conical flasks with fermentation locks in an incubator at 30°C for twenty-four hours.

10. On inspection twenty-four hours later, completion of respiration is evident due to the limewater having now turned milky. In addition, the bubbles of CO_2 can no longer be seen leaving the yeast and glucose solution. The solution which contains the yeast can now be tested to see if it contains ethanol, the other product of anaerobic respiration.

Test for the Presence of Ethanol (Alcohol) (Iodoform Test)

1. Label two test tubes, one as 'Experiment' and the other as 'Control', and set aside in a test tube rack.
2. Label two beakers, one as 'Experiment' and the other as 'Control'.
3. Filter the 'Experiment' and the 'Control' solution into the appropriate beakers, thereby removing as much of the yeast as possible.
4. Place 4 cm^3 of the 'Experiment' filtrate into the test tube labelled 'Experiment'.
5. Place 4 cm^3 of the 'Control' filtrate into the test tube labelled 'Control'.
6. Add 4 cm^3 of potassium iodide solution into each of the above test tubes.
7. Add 6 cm^3 of the sodium hypochlorite solution into each of the above test tubes.
8. Observe and record the appearance of both the test tubes.
9. Using tongs, place both the 'Experiment' and the 'Control' test tubes into a water bath and warm gently for five to six minutes.
10. Allow the water bath to cool and remove the test tubes using the tongs.
11. Observe and record the appearance of both test tubes.
12. Compare the results with those obtained before the test tubes were placed in the water bath.

Results and Observations

	Experiment	Control
Limewater	Turned Milky (therefore CO_2 present)	Remained Clear (therefore no CO_2 present)
Iodoform Test/Test for Alcohol (Exposure to potassium iodide, sodium hypochlorite and gentle heat)	Yellow Crystals Produced (therefore ethanol present)	No Yellow Crystals Produced (therefore no ethanol present)

Control

The control for this experiment is to set up the apparatus without the yeast.

Conclusions

When placed in anaerobic conditions, yeast will produce ethanol and carbon dioxide.

Possible Errors

If the yeast is added to the boiled glucose solution too quickly, the high temperature may denature the enzymes in the yeast.

Difficulty may also arise in ensuring that the glucose solution remains anaerobic for the duration of the experiment.

The anaerobic respiration of yeast is the foundation of the brewing and baking industries. The ethanol produced provides the alcohol for wines and beers. The CO_2 is used in the baking industry to lift the dough in baked goods. The ethanol that is also produced in the cooking process evaporates as a result of the high temperatures in the oven.

Past Exam Questions

2004 Higher Level

Q7 (a) Yeast cells produce ethanol (alcohol) in a process called fermentation. Is this process affected by temperature? Explain your answer.
Yes, this process is affected by temperature. Fermentation is controlled by enzymes, temperature affects the rate of enzyme activity.

(b) Answer the following in relation to an experiment to prepare and show the presence of ethanol using yeast.

Draw a labelled diagram of the apparatus that you used.
See the diagram on p. 82.

Name a substance that yeast can use to make ethanol.
A glucose solution.

What substance other than ethanol is produced during fermentation?
Carbon dioxide is also produced during fermentation.

Describe the control that you used in this experiment.
The control that was used in this experiment was the apparatus set up without the yeast or using yeast that has been killed by boiling.

Explain the purpose of a control in a scientific experiment.
The control provides a comparison against which the actual experiment can be judged. There should only be one variable between the control and the experiment.

How did you know when the fermentation was finished?
It was clear that fermentation was finished when no more bubbles of CO_2 were produced.

Why were solutions of potassium iodide and sodium hypochlorite added to the reaction vessels after a certain period of time?
These chemicals were added to test for the presence of alcohol, a product of anaerobic respiration in yeast.

Name a substance produced during aerobic respiration that is not produced during fermentation.
Water is produced at the end of the electron transport system, which is a part of aerobic respiration. Water is not made during anaerobic respiration.

Questions

1. How were anaerobic conditions achieved in this experiment?
2. What are the two products that are made as a result of anaerobic respiration in yeast cells?
3. For each of the products, name a chemical(s) that test for its presence.
4. How did you know that respiration was completed?
5. What was the control for this experiment?
6. Name two factors that were kept constant during this experiment.
7. Explain how each of the above factors were kept constant.
8. Give a safety precaution that should be followed while performing this experiment.
9. Give a possible error that could occur in this experiment and suggest how it could be avoided.
10. Give an application of the anaerobic respiration of yeast.

Aim

To show an activity in which osmosis takes place and observe the consequences of osmosis. In this experiment, the semi-permeable membrane that is needed for osmosis to take place is visking tubing. This experiment also requires solutions of different concentrations, which in this experiment will be different concentrations of a sucrose solution. The mass of two bags of liquid will be noted before and after this experiment. Any difference in the volume of the bags at the end of the experiment will be as a result of osmosis.

Equipment and Materials

Beakers • distilled water • electronic balance • glass rods • labels • paper towels • scissors • sucrose • syringe • timer • visking tubing • waterproof pen.

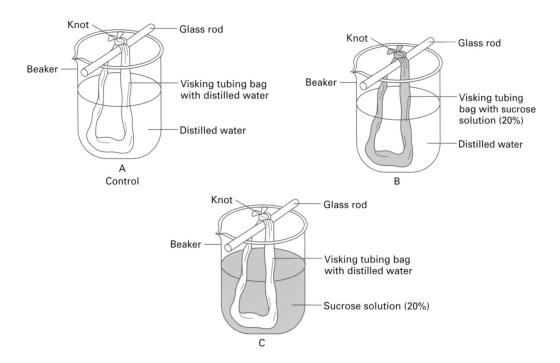

Safety Precautions

Before beginning this experiment, ensure that you have read the procedure thoroughly and have a clear understanding of how to perform the experiment in a safe manner.

Caution should be exercised when using scissors.

Making the Sucrose Solution

1. Make up a 20% sucrose solution by dissolving 40g of sucrose into 200 ml of distilled water.

Demonstrating Osmosis

1. Label three beakers A, B and C.
2. Half fill each of these beakers with the following solutions:
   (a) Distilled water (control).
   (b) Distilled water.
   (c) 20% sucrose solution.
3. Cut three lengths of visking tubing, each 25 cm long.
4. Place three sections of visking tubing into some distilled water to soften it.
5. When the visking tubing is softened, tie a knot at one end of each section.
6. Using a syringe, half fill two of the visking tubes with distilled water and the third tubing with the 20% sucrose solution. Try to remove as much air from the visking tubing as possible and tie a knot in the open ends. (Ensure that there is room in the visking tubing for water to possibly enter.)
7. Wash off any of the sucrose solution from the outside of the third visking tubing and then gently dry using paper towels.
8. Quickly measure the mass of each of the tubes using an electronic balance.
9. Note the fullness (turgidity) of the tubes.
10. Place a visking tube containing distilled water into Beaker A, which contains distilled water. This will be the control.
11. Place the visking tube containing the 20% sucrose solution into Beaker B, which contains distilled water.
12. Place the other visking tube which contains distilled water into Beaker C, which contains the 20% sucrose solution.
13. Suspend each of the visking tubes by tying them around a glass rod that is lying across the top of each beaker.
14. Leave for thirty minutes.
15. Note the size of each of the visking tubes in the beakers.
16. Remove the visking tubes from the beakers, gently dry using paper towels and measure their mass using the electronic balance.

Results and Observations

Beaker	Volume of Visking Tubing at End of Experiment
A	Remained the Same
B	Increased in Size
C	Decreased in Size

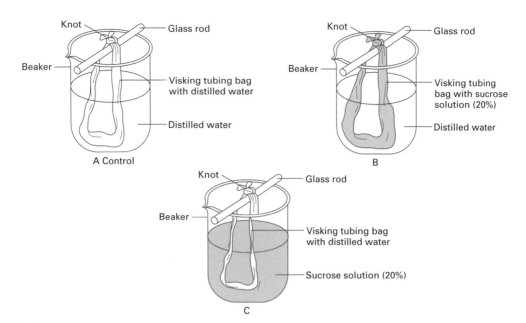

A Control

B

C

Control

The solution in Beaker A was the control, as both of the solutions inside and outside the visking tubing were the same concentration (isotonic).

Conclusions

In Beaker A, the solution outside the visking tubing is the same concentration as the solution in the visking tubing; therefore, there is no net gain or loss of water in the visking tubing.

In Beaker B, the solution outside the visking tubing is less concentrated than the solution in the visking tubing; therefore, more water moves into the visking tubing.

In Beaker C, the solution outside the visking tubing is more concentrated than the solution in the visking tubing; therefore, more water moves out of the visking tubing.

Comments

Students may find it difficult to accurately comment on the turgidity of visking tubing in the beakers at the beginning and end of the experiment. It may be beneficial to take a digital photograph of the size of each of the visking tubings at the beginning and the end of this experiment to accompany the written results.

Possible Errors

The student may overfill the visking tubing, therefore not leaving enough space for liquid to enter into the tubing. This may lead to inaccurate results, showing no increase in the volume of liquid contained by the visking tubing when it is placed into a more dilute solution than that which it contains.

Application

Osmosis can be used to preserve different types of foods. Some foods are surrounded by a high sugar concentration (jams) or salt concentration (meats). This highly concentrated environment causes the water to be drawn from any bacteria that may be on the food and potentially spoiling it. The consequence of this for the micro-organisms is that they become severely dehydrated and therefore will not have enough water in which to carry out important chemical reactions.

Past Exam Questions

2005 Ordinary Level

Q7 (a) (i) What is osmosis?
Osmosis is the movement of water across a semi-permeable membrane from a region of high water concentration to a region of low water concentration.

(ii) What is a selectively permeable (semi-permeable) membrane?
A selectively permeable membrane is a membrane that allows some molecules to pass through while blocking the passage of larger molecules. Examples of selectively permeable membranes are all biological membranes, visking tubing and dialysis tubing.

(b) (i) Draw a labelled diagram of the apparatus that you used to demonstrate osmosis.
See the diagram on p. 87.

(ii) Describe how you carried out the experiment to demonstrate osmosis.
See the procedure on p. 88.

(iii) How were you able to tell that osmosis had taken place?
It was evident that osmosis had taken place because the volume of water contained in the visking tubing (selective permeable membrane) had changed. The visking tubing which was immersed in a more concentrated solution shrank; the visking tube which was immersed in a less concentrated solution swelled; and the visking tube which was immersed in the same concentration liquid stayed the same.

Questions

1. Define osmosis.
2. Explain what is meant by the term 'selectively permeable'.
3. Explain what is meant by the term 'fully permeable'.
4. Explain what is meant by the term 'impermeable'.
5. Name two substances that can pass through a selectively permeable membrane.
6. Name two substances that cannot pass through a selectively permeable membrane.
7. Some visking tubing was half filled with a 25% sucrose solution. The visking tubing was tied and then immersed into a 40% sucrose solution. What change, if any, would happen to the volume of the solution in the visking tubing?
8. What was the control for this experiment?
9. List two ways in which osmosis and diffusion are similar and two ways in which they are different.
10. Give an application of osmosis in industry.

14a Investigate the effect of heat denaturation on the activity of amylase

Aim

To show the effect that exposure to extremes of heat will have on the activity of the enzyme amylase. Some amylase enzyme will be boiled and the rest will remain unboiled. All of these enzymes will then be used in the experiment. Each type will be given optimum conditions for activity, a temperature of 37°C and a pH of 7. By comparing the activity of the boiled and the unboiled enzymes, we can see what the effect of heat denaturation has on the activity of amylase.

Equipment and Materials

Amylase • distilled water • droppers • glass rods • iodine • labels • pH buffer 7 • pH meter • spotting tiles • starch solution • test tube rack • test tubes • test tube holders (or tongs) • thermometer • timer • water bath • waterproof pen.

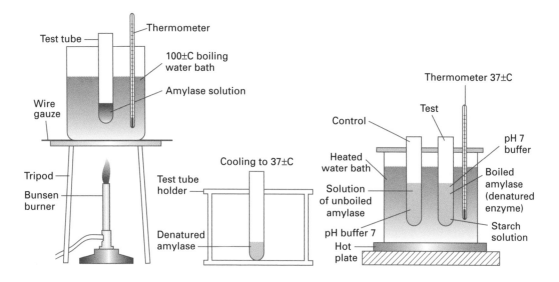

Safety Precautions

Before beginning this experiment, ensure that you have read the procedure thoroughly and have a clear understanding of how to perform the experiment in a safe manner.

Caution should be exercised when using the water bath, as steam and splashes from the boiling water can cause severe burns. If using a Bunsen burner, be extremely cautious of the naked flame.

Iodine is harmful if swallowed, inhaled or if it comes in contact with the skin or eyes. A lab coat, disposable gloves and protective safety glasses should be worn while performing this experiment. Iodine should only be used in a well-ventilated area.

Toxic

Corrosive

Procedure

Prepare the Starch Solution (2%)

1. Prepare the 2% starch solution by placing 2g of soluble starch into a beaker with 100 cm^3 of distilled water.
2. Place the beaker of starch solution into a water bath and set to 100°C.
3. Once the solution has boiled, the starch should be fully dissolved and the solution should be clear. Allow the solution and water bath to cool.
4. If a lot of evaporation has occurred, more distilled water will need to be added to bring the solution back up to 100 cm^3.

Prepare the Amylase Solution (1%)

1. Prepare the 1% amylase solution by placing 1g of soluble amylase powder into a beaker with 100 cm^3 of distilled water.

Investigate the Effect of Heat Denaturation on the Rate of Amylase Activity

1. Set up a water bath at 100°C.
2. Half fill a test tube with some enzyme solution and place it in the boiling water bath for fifteen minutes. This will denature the enzyme.
3. After fifteen minutes, turn off the water bath and allow it to cool. Once cooled, use a test tube holder/tongs to remove the test tube from the water bath.
4. Set up another water bath at 37°C.
5. Label two clean spotting tiles, one as 'Unboiled Amylase at 37°C' and the other as 'Boiled Amylase at 37°C'.
6. Number each of the cavities in the spotting trays (1 to 15). Each cavity represents a one-minute interval.
7. Place these on the bench close to the water bath.
8. Label test tubes with each of the following labels: 'Unboiled Amylase', 'Boiled Amylase', 'Starch', 'Iodine' and 'pH Buffer 7'. Ensure that each test tube is just over half full with its appropriate liquid.
9. Place all of these test tubes in the water bath and allow them to come to 37°C.
10. Label two clean test tubes, one as 'Unboiled Amylase at 37°C' and another as 'Boiled Amylase at 37°C', and place in the water bath.
11. Confirm the temperature using the thermometer.
12. Using a clean pipette, place 4 cm^3 of pH buffer 7 into both the 'Unboiled Amylase' at 37° C and the 'Boiled Amylase' at 37°C.
13. Place 2 cm^3 of amylase into the 'Unboiled Amylase at 37°C' and 2 cm^3 of boiled amylase into the 'Boiled Amylase at 37°C' test tubes.

14. Using a clean pipette, place 4 cm^3 of starch solution into both the 'Unboiled Amylase at 37°C' and the 'Boiled Amylase at 37°C' test tubes.
15. On addition of starch to the solutions in the test tubes, immediately start the timer.
16. Using a clean glass rod each time, stir the contents of the 'Unboiled Amylase at 37°C' and the 'Boiled Amylase at 37°C' test tubes.
17. Place a clean dropper in each of the two test tubes.
18. At one-minute intervals, using their assigned dropper, remove three to four drops of each liquid and place it in the appropriate cavity of the spotting tile.
19. Immediately add a drop of iodine to the drops of solution just placed on the spotting tile. Ensure that you use the clean dropper. Note and record the colours of the solutions.
20. Repeat steps 18 and 19 for fifteen minutes.

Results and Observations

The results of the experiment are as follows.

Enzymes	Time taken for the blue-black colour to disappear
Unboiled Enzyme	Between 5 and 6 minutes.
Boiled Enzyme	The blue-black colour did not disappear.

Control

The control of the experiment is the unboiled enzyme given the optimum conditions of pH 7 and temperature of 37°C.

Conclusions

Denaturing the enzyme by extremes of heat reduced the enzyme's activity to zero. As the unboiled enzyme was shown to be still active, as it had the ability to convert starch to maltose, it can be concluded that boiling the enzyme destroyed its activity.

Comments

The factors that were kept constant in this experiment were pH, temperature, substrate concentration and enzyme concentration. pH was kept constant by using a pH buffer. Temperature was kept constant by using a water bath. Substrate concentration was kept constant by making up a starch solution at the beginning of the experiment and adding the same volume of starch solution to the test tubes each time the experiment was carried out. Enzyme concentration was kept constant by making up an amylase solution at the beginning of the experiment and adding the same volume of amylase solution to the test tubes each time the experiment was carried out.

It is important to note that an enzyme's rate of activity can also be affected by the freshness of the enzyme. As enzymes are protein, they are degraded and broken down over time, which could result in your amylase solution not having the concentration of enzyme you originally thought and therefore possibly not working as quickly as anticipated.

When an enzyme is denatured, its active site has been permanently changed and can no longer fit its substrate; therefore, it can no longer react with it.

Possible Errors

If separate clean pipettes and droppers were not used to transfer the different liquids into the different test tubes, cross-contamination could easily occur. For example, if the same pipette was first used to take up some unboiled amylase solution and then used again to take up some boiled amylase, the boiled amylase could be contaminated with unboiled amylase. Throughout this experiment, pipettes and droppers are used a great deal, so it is important that each pipette and dropper is only used to transfer one particular liquid. There is huge opportunity for cross-contamination if this is not adhered to.

Application

Enzymes have a wide and varied range of applications. As well as being essential for the correct functioning of our bodies, we have also found many important uses for them in the biotechnology industry. In biotechnology, entire organisms, or perhaps just some components (e.g. enzymes), are used to make useful products. We have been using enzymes in the food industry (baking and brewing) for hundreds of years. Today, their use in the food industry has extended and they are used in many different ways. For example, enzymes can be used in fruit juices to make them less cloudy; they are used in slimming products to make them taste sweeter; and they can also be used to help make the gooey centres in some chocolates. One of the largest ways enzymes are sold is in washing detergents. Using enzymes in detergents helps to break down stains, therefore ensuring their successful removal. Also, by using a washing detergent containing enzymes, the wash can be done at a lower temperature, therefore saving energy. Finally, an important use of enzymes is in the medical industry, where they can be used for a wide range of purposes, such as making different antibiotics and helping to treat some diseases.

Questions

1. How was the enzyme denatured in this experiment?
2. Explain what is meant by the term 'denatured'.
3. Give two safety precautions that need to be exercised when carrying out this experiment.
4. What is the optimum pH for the activity of this enzyme?
5. What is the optimum temperature for the activity of this enzyme?
6. What was the control for this experiment?
7. What were the results of this experiment?
8. What conclusions can be drawn from this experiment?
9. Identify a possible error that may be encountered in this experiment.
10. Explain how the possible error mentioned in the previous question could be avoided.

14b Investigate the effect of heat denaturation on the activity of catalase

Aim

To show the effect that exposure to extremes of heat will have on the activity of the enzyme catalase. Some catalase enzymes will be boiled and the rest will remain unboiled. All of these enzymes will then be used in the experiment. Each type will be given optimum conditions for activity, a temperature of 55°C and a pH of 9. By comparing the activity of the boiled and the unboiled enzymes, we can see what effect heat denaturation has on the activity of catalase.

Equipment and Materials

Beakers • boiling tube • catalase, e.g. radishes • chopping board • distilled water • dropper • electronic balance • graduated cylinder • hydrogen peroxide • knife • labels • pH buffer 9 • pH meter • test tube rack • thermometer • tongs • timer • washing-up liquid • water bath • waterproof pen • weigh boat.

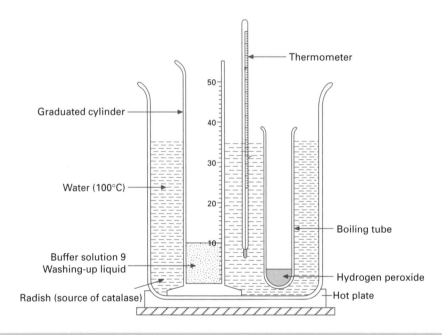

Safety Precautions

Before beginning this experiment, ensure that you have read the procedure thoroughly and have a clear understanding of how to perform the experiment in a safe manner.

Caution should be exercised when using the water bath, as steam and splashes from the boiling water can cause severe burns.

Hydrogen peroxide is corrosive and can cause burns if it comes in contact with the skin or eyes. It is also harmful if inhaled or ingested. When handling hydrogen peroxide, always wear safety glasses and appropriate protective gloves.

Harmful

Corrosive

Procedure

1. Set a water bath to a temperature of 55°C.
2. Using the knife, finely chop the radish on the chopping board.
3. Label a graduated cylinder as 'Experiment' and place it in the water bath.
4. Label a boiling tube with 'pH Buffer 9'. Using a clean pipette, place 15 cm^3 of pH buffer 9 into this boiling tube.
5. Label a boiling tube as 'Washing-up Liquid'. Using a clean pipette, add a small amount (1–2 cm^3) of washing-up liquid to this boiling tube.
6. Label a boiling tube as 'Hydrogen Peroxide'. Using a clean pipette, place 3 cm^3 of hydrogen peroxide into this boiling tube.
7. Label a boiling tube as 'Radish Catalase'. Using an electronic balance and clean spatula, measure out and place 5g of finely chopped radish into this boiling tube.
8. Allow all of the items placed in the water bath to come to the correct temperature.
9. Once they have reached the correct temperature, use tongs to pour the test tube of pH buffer into the graduated cylinder.
10. Transfer the 5g finely chopped radish into the graduated cylinder labelled 'Experiment'.
11. Using a clean dropper, add one drop of washing-up liquid into the graduated cylinder.
12. Finally, using tongs, pour the boiling tube of the hydrogen peroxide into the graduated cylinder.
13. On addition of the hydrogen peroxide, immediately note the volume of the liquid in the graduated cylinder and begin the timer.
14. After two minutes, observe and record the volume of the liquid in the graduated cylinder.
15. Repeat steps 1 to 14 but this time boil the chopped radish and allow it to cool before using it in the experiment.

Results and Observations

Enzymes	Foam produced?
Unboiled Enzyme	Yes, therefore the enzyme is active
Boiled Enzyme	No, therefore the enzyme is denatured

Control

The control of the experiment is the unboiled enzyme given the optimum conditions of pH 9 and temperature 55°C.

Conclusions

Denaturing the enzyme by extremes of heat reduced the enzyme's activity to zero. As the unboiled enzyme was shown to be still active, as it had the ability to convert hydrogen peroxide to water and oxygen, it can be concluded that boiling the enzyme destroyed its activity.

Comments

The factors that were kept constant in this experiment were pH, temperature, substrate concentration and enzyme concentration. pH was kept constant by using a pH buffer. Temperature was kept constant by using a water bath. Substrate concentration was kept constant by adding a set volume of hydrogen peroxide to the experiment each time the experiment was carried out. Enzyme concentration was kept constant by adding the same amount of finely chopped radish each time the experiment was carried out.

It is important to note that an enzyme's rate of activity can also be affected by the freshness of the enzyme. As enzymes are protein, they are degraded and broken down over time, which could result in your catalase solution not having the concentration of enzyme you originally thought and therefore possibly not working as quickly as anticipated.

When an enzyme is denatured, its active site has been permanently changed and can no longer fit its substrate; therefore, it can no longer react with it.

Possible Errors

If the volume of the fluid in the graduated cylinder is not measured immediately, the true volume of the foam produced may not be correctly measured and therefore an inaccurate final result may be produced.

The amount of time that each experiment is given to produce foam must also be consistent so that the same parameters are applied to each experiment.

The washing-up liquid must be added to the enzyme before the substrate so that all of the product released can be measured. If it is added after the substrate, some of the oxygen will have already been released and the column of foam may not reach its full potential.

It must be noted that, in this experiment, it is more important to observe whether or not the foam was produced rather than measuring the exact volume produced.

Application

Enzymes have a wide and varied range of applications. As well being essential for the correct functioning of our bodies, we have also found many important uses for them in the biotechnology industry. In biotechnology, entire organisms, or perhaps just some components of organisms (e.g. enzymes), are used to make useful products. We have been using enzymes in the food industry (baking and brewing) for hundreds of years. Today, their use in the food industry has extended and they are used in many different ways. For example, enzymes can be used in fruit juices to make them less cloudy; they are used in slimming products to make them taste sweeter; and they can also be used to help make the gooey centres in some chocolates. One of the largest ways enzymes are sold is in washing detergents. Using enzymes in detergents helps to break down stains, therefore ensuring their successful removal. Also, by using a washing detergent containing enzymes, the wash can be done at a lower temperature, therefore saving energy. Finally, an important use of enzymes is in the medical industry, where they can be used for a wide range of purposes, such as making different antibiotics and helping to treat some diseases.

Questions

1. What are the substrate and products of catalase?
2. Name two possible sources of the enzyme catalase.
3. What is meant when an enzyme is described as being denatured?
4. How was the enzyme denatured in this experiment?
5. What was the control in this experiment?
6. How was the rate of enzyme activity measured?
7. What is the function of the washing-up liquid in this experiment?
8. Give a possible error that may occur in this experiment and explain how it may be avoided.
9. Give a safety precaution that should be followed when carrying out this experiment.
10. Give an application of the use of enzymes in modern technology.

15 Isolate DNA from a plant tissue

Aim

To isolate the DNA from onion cells. Each step of the experiment will break down or remove a part of the cell until just the DNA remains. The final step will be the extraction of the DNA from the solution.

Equipment and Materials

Beakers • blender • boiling tube • chopping board • coffee filter paper • disposable gloves • electronic balance • ethanol (ice cold) • distilled water • droppers • funnel • glass rod • graduated cylinder • knife • onion • protease, e.g. trypsin • salt • spatula • syringe • test tube rack • thermometer • timer • washing-up liquid • water bath • weigh boat.

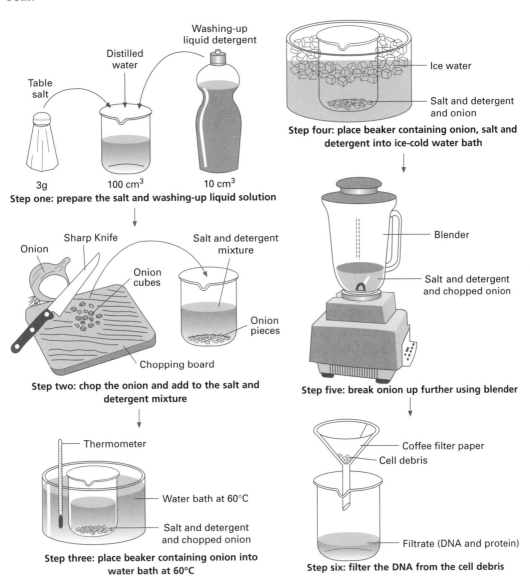

Washing-up liquid detergent

Distilled water

Table salt

3g   100 cm³   10 cm³

Step one: prepare the salt and washing-up liquid solution

Ice water

Salt and detergent and onion

Step four: place beaker containing onion, salt and detergent into ice-cold water bath

Sharp Knife

Onion

Onion cubes

Salt and detergent mixture

Onion pieces

Chopping board

Step two: chop the onion and add to the salt and detergent mixture

Blender

Salt and detergent and chopped onion

Step five: break onion up further using blender

Thermometer

Water bath at 60°C

Salt and detergent and chopped onion

Step three: place beaker containing onion into water bath at 60°C

Coffee filter paper

Cell debris

Filtrate (DNA and protein)

Step six: filter the DNA from the cell debris

99

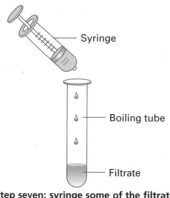

Syringe

Boiling tube

Filtrate

Step seven: syringe some of the filtrate into a boiling tube

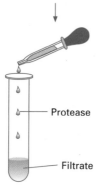

Protease

Filtrate

Step eight: add a protease to break down the protein surrounding DNA

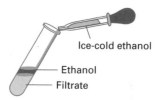

Ice-cold ethanol

Ethanol

Filtrate

Step nine: carefully add a layer of ice-cold ethanol over the filtrate

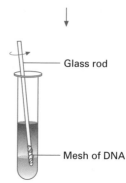

Glass rod

Mesh of DNA

Step ten: collect the DNA using a glass rod

Safety Precautions

Before beginning this experiment, ensure that you have read the procedure thoroughly and have a clear understanding of how to perform the experiment in a safe manner.

Caution should be exercised when using the water bath, as steam and splashes from the hot water can cause severe burns.

Ethanol is highly flammable and therefore needs to be used away from sources of heat and in a well-ventilated area. Irritation is caused if it comes in contact with the eyes, so safety glasses must be worn.

Highly flammable

Harmful

Caution should be exercised when using sharp blades. The cutting should always be done on a chopping board and the direction of the cutting should be away from the person's body.

Procedure

1. Cut the onion into small cubes so that the there is a large enough surface area for the chemicals to work, thereby ensuring a greater chance of collecting the DNA successfully.
2. Using a clean spatula, place 3g of salt into a large beaker.
3. Measure 10 cm^3 of washing-up liquid and add to the salt in the large beaker.
4. Bring this solution up to 100 cm^3 using distilled water.
5. Place the cut onion cubes into this solution and stir gently.
6. Place the beaker in a water bath at 60°C for fifteen minutes.
7. After fifteen minutes, remove the beaker from the warm water bath and place into an ice water bath for five minutes, stirring gently throughout this time.
8. After five minutes, remove the beaker from the ice water bath and pour the contents into a standard food blender.
9. Turn the food blender on for no more than three seconds.
10. Set up a large beaker with a large funnel lined with coffee filter paper.
11. Filter the blended solution through the coffee filter paper.
12. Once filtration is finished, remove 15 cm^3 of the filtrate and place into a boiling tube.
13. Add three to four drops of a protease enzyme, e.g. trypsin, into the filtrate in the boiling tube.
14. Remove the ethanol from the freezer and gently pour 10–15 cm^3 down the side of the boiling tube so that a layer of ethanol is formed on top of the filtrate.
15. Gently place the boiling tube in a test tube rack. Observe where the filtrate and the ethanol meet and leave to settle for five minutes.
16. After five minutes, observe where the filtrate and the ethanol meet and note any changes.
17. Gently place a clean glass rod in the boiling tube to at least the point at which the two liquids meet. Stir the rod gently and collect the DNA.
18. Record your observations and results.

Results and Observations

A clear mass of threads can be seen at the point where the filtrate and the ice-cold ethanol meet. These threads of DNA can then be collected by the glass rod and observed outside of the boiling tube.

Control

There is no control for this experiment.

Conclusions

Onion cells contain DNA, which when isolated appears as clear, sticky threads.

Comments

The washing-up liquid was used in this experiment to break up the cells' membranes by causing their lipids and proteins to break apart. Breaking up the cells' membranes releases the DNA from the nucleus.

The salt in this experiment is required to prevent the DNA from being attracted to the proteins from the cells' membranes, as this would add to the difficulty of isolating the DNA. As a result of the salt, the DNA is no longer attracted to the proteins and the DNA then starts to clump together.

When cells become damaged, as would have occurred by chopping and adding washing-up liquid to our onion, enzymes in the cells are released that digest the broken remains of the cell. As we are trying to isolate the DNA, we do not want it to be digested by the DNases (enzymes that digest DNA) released by damaging the cell. By heating the solution at 60°C, the enzymes that would digest the DNA are denatured. However, if the solution is left at 60°C for longer than fifteen minutes, the DNA itself would be broken down by the high temperatures.

Cooling the solution in the ice water bath helps to prevent the breakdown of the DNA by the higher temperatures. The cold temperature also slows the activity of any DNases that may not have been denatured by the high temperatures.

The blending of the solution for three seconds breaks down the cell walls and further breaks down the cells' membranes. This results in the DNA being fully released from the cells. However, if the solution is blended for more than three seconds, the DNA itself is shredded.

Filtering the solution allows the DNA to be separated from the other broken remains of the cells. The coffee filter paper has larger pores than regular laboratory filter paper and thus allows the process of filtration to happen at a more acceptable rate for the experiment while still separating the DNA from the rest of the cell remains.

A protease is a protein-digesting enzyme. In this experiment, it is used to break down the proteins that the DNA wraps around in the nucleus, i.e. histones. It is best to use a protease whose optimum pH is around 7 and which can function at room temperature. Trypsin is a good option, but pineapple juice can also be used as a source of protease enzymes.

The ethanol removes water from the DNA, which results in the DNA being lighter, so it floats up to where the filtrate and the ethanol meet. The ethanol has to be ice cold, as this causes the DNA to be insoluble. Therefore, the DNA can now be seen. If the ethanol is at room temperature, the DNA will be soluble in the ethanol and therefore cannot be seen.

Possible Errors

As seen in the Comments section above, many of the steps in this experiment involve the breaking down of enzymes, cell membranes and cell walls. If any of these steps that involve breaking down materials continue for longer than they are supposed to, it is very likely that the DNA will also be destroyed and, therefore, be unavailable to be isolated.

Application

The isolation of DNA has many applications in today's scientific world. When DNA is isolated from a person's cell, it can be used to make a pattern of bands that is unique to that person. This DNA profile can be critical in crime scene investigations, as the isolated DNA taken from cells that are found at the scenes of crimes often provides essential evidence to uncover the guilty party. DNA profiles are also used to help identify a person's biological parents. Another use of DNA is genetic screening. This is where a person's DNA is examined for faulty genes and is used to provide people with information on their risk of having a child with a particular condition.

2006 Higher Level

Q7 (b) (iii) In the case of each of the following, state:

(1) An investigation in which you used it.

(2) The precise purpose for its use in the investigation that you have indicated.
Cold alcohol (ethanol).
1. To isolate DNA from a plant tissue.
2. The ethanol helps to separate and isolate the DNA from the solution it is in. The ethanol removes water from the DNA, which results in the DNA becoming lighter, so it floats up to where the filtrate and the ethanol meet. The ethanol has to be ice cold, as this causes the DNA to be insoluble.

2005 Higher Level

Q8 (a) Explain each of the following terms in relation to DNA.

(i) Replication.
Replication refers to DNA making an exact copy of itself.

(ii) Transcription.
Transcription refers to the copying of DNA into a strand of RNA.

(b) As part of your practical activities, you extracted DNA from a plant tissue. Answer the following questions in relation to this experiment.

(i) What plant did you use?
An onion.

(ii) It is usual to chop the tissue and place it in a blender. Suggest a reason for this.
The tissue was placed in the blender to break up the cell walls and therefore release the cytoplasm.

(iii) For how long should the blender be allowed to run?
For three seconds.

(iv) Washing-up liquid is normally used in this experiment. What is its function?
The function of washing-up liquid is to break down the cell membrane by breaking down the lipids and causing the proteins to break apart. By breaking down the cell membrane, the nucleic acid is released.

(v) Sodium chloride (salt) is also used. Explain why.
Sodium chloride is used to cause the DNA to clump together. It does this by helping to separate the DNA from the proteins of the membranes.

(vi) What is a protease enzyme?
A protease enzyme is one that breaks down protein.

(vii) Why is a protease enzyme used in this experiment?

A protease enzyme is used in this experiment to break down the protein (histones) around the DNA.

(viii) The final separation of the DNA involves the use of alcohol (ethanol). Under what conditions is the alcohol used?

The ethanol needs to be ice-cold, as DNA is insoluble in ice-cold ethanol.

Questions

1. Why was the onion in this experiment cut into small cubes?
2. What was the function of the washing-up liquid in this experiment?
3. What was the function of the salt in this experiment?
4. Why was the blender used in this experiment?
5. How long was the blender turned on for? Explain why it was only turned on for this length of time.
6. Why is coffee filter paper used instead of laboratory filter paper?
7. What passes through into the filtrate and what remains behind in the filter paper?
8. What is the function of a protease enzyme? Give an example of one.
9. What is the function of the ice-cold ethanol?
10. Give a safety precaution that should be followed when carrying out this experiment.

16 Investigate the growth of leaf yeast using agar plates and controls

Aim

To show that micro-organisms (yeast) are unseen yet present on leaves. We will show this by growing colonies of the yeast that fall from the leaves onto nutrient agar plates. To ensure the validity of our results, aseptic techniques have to be rigidly followed.

Equipment and Materials

Alcohol • Bunsen burner • disinfectant • forceps • incubator • inoculation loop • labels • leaves (ash) • malt agar dishes • matches • paper towels • petroleum jelly • secateurs/scissors • sterile container (as clean as possible) • waterproof pen.

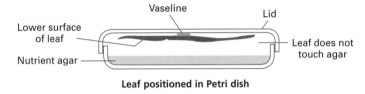

Leaf positioned in Petri dish

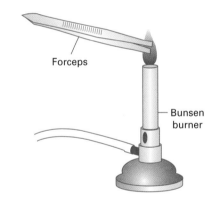

Flaming equipment to sterilise it

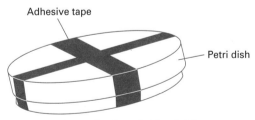

A completely sealed Petri dish

Safety Precautions

Before beginning this experiment, ensure that you have read the procedure thoroughly and have a clear understanding of how to perform the experiment in a safe manner.

Ethanol is highly flammable and therefore needs to be used away from sources of heat and in a well-ventilated area. Irritation is caused if it comes in contact with the eyes, so safety glasses must be worn.

In this experiment, a Bunsen burner is used to sterilise the forceps and the inoculation loop before and after they have been used. As the burner will be on over the entire duration of the experiment, extreme caution is needed to prevent burns.

Procedure

1. Using a secateurs, gather leaves from the tree and place four leaves in a clean plastic container. When collecting the leaves, try not to touch them directly with your fingers.
2. Disinfect the bench and fill a beaker with approximately 30 ml of alcohol and leave to one side.
3. Light the Bunsen burner and leave on a low flame a safe distance from the beaker of alcohol.
4. Open the plastic container.
5. Take the forceps in one hand and sterilise it by passing it through the flame of the Bunsen burner.
6. Using the forceps, remove a leaf from the bag.
7. If the leaves are too big to fit across the Petri dish, sterilise the scissors and use them to cut the leaves to a more suitable size.
8. While still holding the leaf in the forceps with one hand, use your other hand to pick up the inoculating loop and sterilise it by passing it through the flame of the Bunsen burner.
9. Use the inoculation loop to lift a piece of petroleum jelly and place it on the upper side of the leaf.
10. When the petroleum jelly is off the inoculation loop, sterilise it again by flaming it and then place it on the bench.
11. Still holding the leaf and the forceps in one hand, use the other hand to quickly open an agar plate. Stick the leaf to the lid of the agar plate using the petroleum jelly. When the leaf is in place, immediately close the agar plate. Ensure that the leaf is not touching the agar.
12. Flame the forceps and place on the bench.
13. Seal the Petri dish and label its underside as 'Unsterilised Leaf'.
14. For the control in this experiment, repeat steps 4 to 13 with a second leaf, but with the following changes:

Before the petroleum jelly is placed on the leaf, sterilise the leaf by washing it in the beaker of alcohol. Also ensure that you label these agar plates as 'Controls'.

15. Leave all the plates right way up for one day and then invert them. This allows the yeast enough time to fall from the leaves and onto the nutrient agar. The plates are inverted to prevent condensation from forming.

16. Place all the agar plates in an incubator at 25°C for three to four days.

17. After three or four days, remove the agar plates from the incubator and observe the results.

18. When the experiment is complete immerse all of the agar plates used, the forceps and the inoculation loop in disinfectant overnight. The disposable items may then be placed in a bin. Disinfect the bench.

Results and Observations

There is yeast growing on the agar in the agar plates with the unsterilised leaves. The yeast colonies appear as small pink to red circles, and as they have fallen from the leaf, they will grow on the agar in the shape of the leaf.

The result in the agar plates with the sterilised leaves is that there is no yeast growing on the agar.

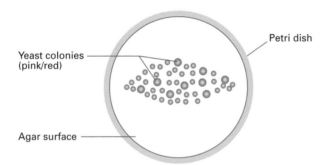

Yeast colonies growing on agar

Control

The control for this experiment is the agar plates with the sterilised leaves in them.

Conclusions

There is yeast present on the underside of the ash leaves.

Possible Errors

If an aseptic technique is not used, the sterilised leaves could become contaminated with yeast and other micro-organisms, therefore giving false results.

If the leaves placed in the Petri dishes are touching the agar, other micro-organisms, such as bacteria, can make it down onto the agar and begin to grow on it, possibly obscuring your yeast colony results.

The undersurface of the leaves are exposed to the agar as there are more micro-organisms found on the sheltered underside of the leaves.

The growth of leaf yeast is often used as an indicator as to the air quality of an area. The less leaf yeast, the greater the level of air pollution. The leaves of trees on the edge of a main road would have less leaf yeast than a tree in the middle of an isolated country field.

2007 Higher Level

Q8 (a) (i) Name a fungus, other than yeast, that you studied during your course.
             Rhizopus, otherwise known as bread mould.

        (ii) Give one way in which the fungus that you have named in (i) differs from yeast.
              Rhizopus is a multi-cellular organism made up of thread-like hyphae, whereas yeast is unicellular.

    (b) Answer the following questions in relation to your investigation of the growth of leaf yeast.

        (i) It was necessary to use a nutrient medium. What is a nutrient medium?
             A nutrient medium is a material on which the yeast can grow, as it provides a supply of food necessary for the yeast.

        (ii) Name the nutrient medium that you used.
              Malt agar.

        (iii) The nutrient medium should be <u>sterile</u>. Explain the underlined term.
               The word 'sterile' means to be completely free of micro-organisms.

        (iv) Describe, in words and/or labelled diagram(s), how you conducted the investigation.
              See the procedure and diagrams on pages 105–107.

        (v) What was the result of your investigation?
             The result of the investigation is that there were red or pink colonies of yeast growing on the agar of the plate containing the untreated leaf, while there were no colonies growing on the agar of the plates containing the control leaf.

2005 Higher Level

Q9 (a) (i) Yeasts are eukaryotic organisms. What does this mean?
             An organism that is described as being eukaryotic contains a distinct nucleus and membrane-bound organelles, e.g. mitochondria.

        (ii) To which kingdom do yeasts belong?
              Fungi.

    (b) Answer the following questions in relation to an experiment that you carried out to investigate the growth of leaf yeast.

        (i) From which plant did you collect the leaf sample?
             An ash tree.

(ii)   Describe how you collected the leaf sample.
The leaf was cut from the tree and placed directly into a clean container. The leaf blade was not touched directly to prevent any contamination.

(iii) What did you do with the leaves when you returned to the laboratory?
The leaves were kept sealed in their container until the experiment began. While performing the experiment, the leaves were handled using only a sterile forceps. These two steps were necessary to avoid contamination from an outside source. In the experiment, some petroleum jelly was placed on the upper surface of the leaf in order for it to stick to the lid of the Petri dish. The leaves in the agar plates were left in an incubator at 25°C for the following three to four days.

(iv)   Nutrient agar plates are used in this experiment. What are nutrient agar plates and what is their purpose?
Nutrient agar plates are Petri dishes that contain a solid gel containing a food supplement that will provide nutrition for micro-organisms to grow.

(v)   What did you observe in the agar plates at the end of the experiment?
There were pink or red circles growing on the agar plates at the end of the experiment.

(vi)   Having finished the experiment, what did you do with the agar plates?
On completion of the experiment, the agar plates were sterilised by immersing them in a disinfectant for twenty-four hours and then placing in the bin.

Questions

1. What is meant by the term 'aseptic'?
2. Give three different aseptic techniques that were used during this experiment.
3. Describe how the leaves were placed into the agar plates.
4. Why was the underside of the leaf facing the nutrient agar instead of the upper surface?
5. Why should you not let the leaf come into contact with the agar?
6. Why were the agar plates inverted during this experiment?
7. Describe the appearance of the yeast colonies.
8. What was the control in this experiment and what result can be seen in this plate?
9. Explain how you can safely dispose of the agar plates after the experiment is complete.
10. Give a safety precaution that you would follow while carrying out this experiment.

17 **Prepare and examine microscopically the transverse section of a dicotyledonous stem (×100, ×400)**

Aim

To prepare a slide of a transverse section of a dicotyledonous stem. This slide then has to be successfully viewed using a light microscope. The slide can be viewed without a stain, but a stain can be used if a clearer image is required.

Equipment and Materials

Chopping board • cover slips • dicotyledonous plant stem (sunflower/busy lizzy/buttercup) • distilled water • droppers • forceps • glass microscope slides • light microscope • paintbrush (small) • Petri dish • scalpel • seeker (for lowering the cover slip) • test tube rack • test tubes • tissue paper.

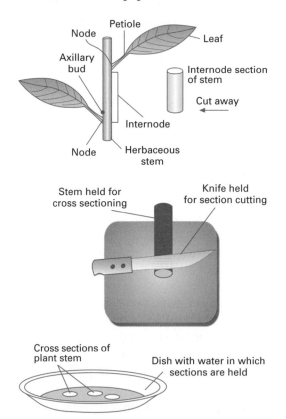

Safety Precautions

Before beginning this experiment, ensure that you have read the procedure thoroughly and have a clear understanding of how to perform the experiment in a safe manner.

Caution should be exercised when using sharp blades. The cutting should always be done on a chopping board and the direction of the cutting should be away from the person's body.

1. Set up the microscope, ensuring that the light source is providing adequate light.
2. Label a test tube as 'Distilled Water'. Place this test tube one-third full into the test tube rack.
3. Half fill the Petri dish with water and place on the bench. The cut sections of the sunflower/busy lizzy/buttercup stem will be stored here to prevent them from drying out.
4. Place your chosen stem on the chopping board and carefully cut thin cross-sections using the wetted blade of a scalpel.
5. Store the cut sections of stem in the Petri dish of water.
6. Place a glass slide flat on the bench. Using a dropper, place one drop of distilled water on the slide.
7. Using the forceps or a small paintbrush, place one thin cross-section of the stem on the glass slide.
8. Using the seeker as an aid, place a cover slip over the stem on the slide. The cover slip should be dropped slowly at an angle (45°) so that the air will be pushed out and will not be trapped under the cover slip, possibly obscuring your view of the cells.
9. If there is excess liquid on the slide, gently soak up the excess by placing a clean corner of tissue or filter paper on the excess liquid.
10. Move the lenses of the microscope away from the stage.
11. Place the slide on the stage with the section of stem over the light source and secure into place using the clips.
12. Ensure that the low-power lens is over the sample and then, while looking at the microscope from the side, lower the lens as close as possible over the slide without touching the lens off the slide.
13. Now looking through the eyepiece, bring the stem into focus by slowly moving the lens away from the slide.
14. When the stem and its vascular bundles can be seen, bring them into sharp focus using the fine focus wheel.
15. Record your results by drawing what the stem and its vascular bundles look like at this magnification (×100).
16. When the stem and its vascular bundles have been observed and drawn at this magnification, use the nosepiece to place the higher-power lens over the slide. Do not adjust the height of the lens, as once the stem is in focus with the low-power lens, it should still be in focus when the higher-power lens is used and only minor adjustments to sharpen the image are all that should be necessary.
17. Record you results by drawing what the stem and its vascular bundles look like at this magnification (×400). No extra detail will be seen – the stem and vascular bundles will just look bigger.
18. When you have finished your drawings and are done with the slide, move the lenses away from the slide and remove this slide.

Results and Observations

A circular vascular bundle arrangement in a dicotyledonous stem was visible using the light microscope.

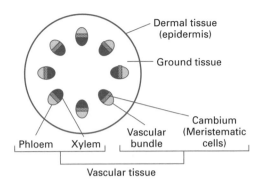

Dermal tissue (epidermis)

Ground tissue

Cambium (Meristematic cells)

Vascular bundle

Phloem   Xylem

Vascular tissue

Control

There is no control for this experiment.

Conclusions

Light microscopes allowed us to see that the vascular bundle arrangement in a dicotyledonous stem is circular.

Comments

If using the sunflower stem, examine its cut end and note that the circular arrangement of the vascular bundles can already be clearly observed, even without using the microscope.

It is not a requirement that the transverse section of the dicotyledonous stem be viewed stained, though this will improve the clarity of the parts of this stem. The following are suggested stains.

- **Aniline sulphate:** This stains lignin a yellow colour; therefore, the xylem will appear yellow.
- **Iodine:** This stains starch blue-black and lignin walls a yellow-gold colour.
- **Toluidine blue:** This stains xylem a green-turquoise colour and dermal and ground tissue a purple colour.

The xylem will always be towards the centre of the stem, with the phloem always towards the outer dermal section of the stem.

As with any experiment involving stains, be careful when using them not to allow them to come in contact with your skin, do not use excess and allow a few minutes for the stain to be absorbed into the cells for best results.

Iodine is harmful if swallowed, inhaled or if it comes in contact with the skin or eyes. A lab coat, disposable gloves and protective safety glasses should be worn while performing this experiment. Iodine should only be used in a well-ventilated area.

Toxic

Corrosive

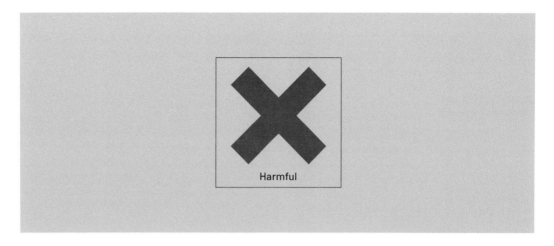

Harmful

Wetting the blade can often make the cutting of thin sections more successful, as there is a smoother movement of the blade.

If it is too difficult to cut a thin enough slice of the stem, a microtome can be used. A microtome is a piece of equipment that is used for cutting very thin sections of tissue for viewing under the microscope. An easy way to make something similar is to remove the centre of a carrot and place the stem in this central space. Keep the stem just over the edge of the carrot and using the blade, cut a very thin slice off both the stem and the carrot.

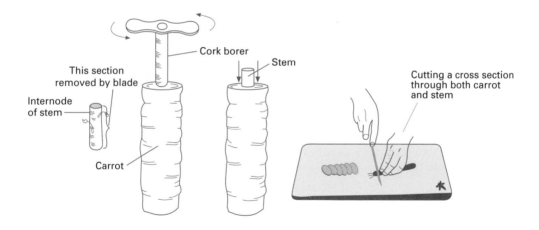

Possible Errors

When using the microscope, the cells may be brought into focus by moving the lens down towards the cells while viewing through the eyepiece. The problem with this method is that as you are looking through the eyepiece, you cannot see how close the lens is to the slide and if you miss the point where the cells are in focus (which can often happen if you are moving the lens too quickly or if you blinked and missed them), you may end up pushing the lens through the cover slip of the slide. If this happens, you have ruined you slide and will have to prepare it again, but, more importantly, you may have ruined the lens. The correct way to focus on cells is to look at the lenses from the side, bring the lens down as close as possible to the slide without touching it and then bring the cells into focus by moving the lens away from the slide.

Another possible error is that the stem section could be cut too thick. As a result, too little light will get through and therefore the sample cannot be seen.

Application

Histology is the study of cells using a microscope. Research into plant cells' structures and functions are ongoing and the microscope plays an invaluable role in this. By knowing what healthy plant tissue and cells are supposed to look like under microscopes, we can therefore also identify abnormal plant tissue and cells. This is important in diagnosing different types of plant diseases. Microscopes would also be required in the area of plant tissue culture, for example.

Past Exam Questions

2004 Higher Level

Q8 (a) Observation of a transverse section of a dicotyledonous stem reveals vascular and other tissues. Name two of the tissues that are not vascular tissues.
Dermal and ground tissues.

(b) Answer the following questions in relation to the preparation of a microscope slide of a transverse section of a dicotyledonous stem.

State one reason why you used a herbaceous stem rather than a woody one.
The herbaceous stem is much easier to cut into thin sections compared with a woody stem.

Explain how you cut the section.
The stem was cut by firstly using a backed blade. A scalpel was used to cut the stem between two nodes, then the backed blade, scalpel or a microtome can be used to cut the stem into thin sections. Great care is required when using sharp blades.

Why is it desirable to cut the section as thinly as possible?
It is desirable to cut the section as thinly as possible so that light can make it through the stem into the microscope lens so that it can be seen clearly.

Draw a diagram of the section as seen under the microscope. Label the vascular tissues that can be seen.
See the diagram on p. 112.

State one precise function of each of the vascular tissues labelled in your diagram.
Phloem is used to transport food and auxins. Xylem is used to transport water and minerals.

Questions

1. Give an example of two different plants that can be used as a dicotyledonous stem.
2. Explain how a thin section of the dicotyledonous stem was obtained.

3. Explain why the thinly cut sections of the stem are placed in a Petri dish containing water.
4. Suggest a stain that could be used if a clearer view of the dicotyledonous stem is required.
5. Draw a diagram of the cover slip being placed on the transverse section of the stem.
6. Give a safety precaution that is required to carry out this experiment.
7. Name the three types of tissues that can be seen in the dicotyledonous stem.
8. Give a possible error that could arise in this experiment.
9. Explain how this error could be avoided.
10. Draw a diagram of the cross-section of the stem that you viewed.

TITLE 18 Dissect, display and identify an ox's or a sheep's heart

Aim

To perform a successful dissection of a sheep's heart, after which all the major external and internal features of the heart should be clearly identifiable.

Equipment and Materials

Disinfectant • dissection board • dissection kit • dropper • dye • flag pin labels • forceps • paper towel • pencil • rubber gloves • scalpel • scissors • seekers • sheep's heart.

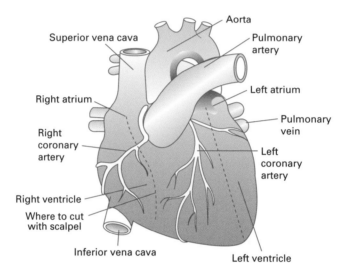

External view of heart

Safety Precautions

Before beginning this experiment, ensure that you have read the procedure thoroughly and have a clear understanding of how to perform the experiment in a safe manner.

Caution should be exercised when using sharp blades. The cutting should always be done on a dissection board and the direction of the cutting should be away from the person's body.

Gloves should be worn throughout this experiment.

Procedure

1. Using a pencil, prepare all the flag labels prior to the dissection and arrange them close to the dissection board.
2. Wash the heart as thoroughly as possible using cold water and dry the heart with paper towels.
3. Place the heart on the dissection board.

4. Identify the front (ventral) side from the back (dorsal) side. The front of the heart can be identified by feeling the ventricle wall's thickness. The left side of the heart has a thicker wall and will feel thicker and stronger to the touch. Also, the coronary vessel can be seen running diagonally from left to right on the front of the heart.

5. Draw a labelled diagram of the external view of the heart before the dissection begins. Identify where the chambers of the heart and the exterior blood vessels are located.

6. Using a scalpel, carefully make a long cut down the heart to the left of the septum.

7. When cut, open the heart widely so that all the interior of the left side of the heart can be seen.

8. Clean the interior of the heart with cold water if necessary.

9. Using seekers or gloved fingers, note each of the following features of the left side of the heart.

    (a) The difference in size of the chambers of the left atrium and ventricle.

    (b) The thickness of the left ventricle wall in general and in comparison to the thickness of the left atrium wall.

    (c) The valve between the left atrium and the left ventricle. This valve has two flaps and is accordingly called the bicuspid valve.

    (d) The chordae tendinae (heart strings) which extend from the bicuspid valve to the papillary muscles in the left ventricle walls.

    (e) Note that the blood vessels that enter into the left atrium are the pulmonary veins.

    (f) Note that the blood vessel exiting at the top of the left ventricle is the aorta. There is a valve at the base of this artery – this is the semilunar valve.

    (g) At the base of the aorta above the semilunar valve, there are two small openings. These are the entries into the coronary arteries which supply the heart muscle with oxygen and nutrients. To observe the coronary arteries in more detail, dye or air can be gently pumped into them using a dropper.

10. Repeat steps 6 to 8 on the right side of the heart. Note each of the following features of the right side of the heart.

    (a) The difference in size of the chambers of the right atrium and ventricle.

    (b) The thickness of the right ventricle wall and how it compares to the walls of the right atrium and the left ventricle.

    (c) The valve between the right ventricle and the right atrium. This valve has three flaps and is accordingly called the tricuspid valve.

    (d) The chordae tendinae which extend from the tricuspid valve to the papillary muscles in the right ventricle walls.

    (e) Note that the blood vessels that enter into the right atrium are the superior and inferior venae cavae.

    (f) Note that the blood vessel exiting at the top of the right ventricle is the pulmonary artery. There is a valve at the base of this artery – this is another semilunar valve.

    (g) Note the thick wall, called the septum, that separates the left side of the heart from the right side.

11. Using the flag pin labels, label all the parts of the heart that you have identified.

12. Draw a diagram of the dissected heart.

13. Sterilise all the dissecting equipment and the dissection board using a disinfectant.

Results and Observations

The following parts of the heart are to be identified:

- Left atrium
- Left ventricle
- Right atrium
- Right ventricle
- Aorta
- Pulmonary artery
- Pulmonary veins (×2)
- Superior vena cava
- Inferior vena cava
- Bicuspid valve (two flaps of tissue)
- Tricuspid valve (three flaps of tissue)
- Semilunar valve (two flaps of tissue)
- Papillary muscles
- Tendons/Chordae Tendinae
- Thickened left ventricle wall
- Septum
- Coronary arteries
- Pericardium (possibly)

	Right Side	Left Side
Atria Size	Small	Small
Atria Wall Thickness	Thin	Thin
Ventricle Size	Large	Large
Ventricle Wall Thickness	Thin	Thick
Valve between Atrium and Ventricle (Number of Flaps)	Tricuspid valve (3)	Bicuspid valve (2)
Valve Exiting the Ventricle (Number of Flaps)	Semilunar valve (3)	Semilunar valve (3)

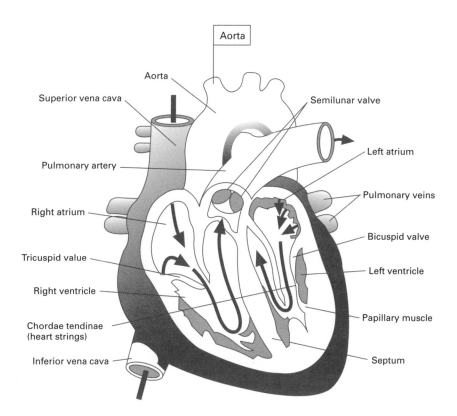

Aorta

Aorta

Superior vena cava

Semilunar valve

Pulmonary artery

Left atrium

Right atrium

Pulmonary veins

Tricuspid value

Bicuspid valve

Right ventricle

Left ventricle

Chordae tendinae
(heart strings)

Papillary muscle

Inferior vena cava

Septum

Control

There is no control for this experiment.

Conclusions

The dissection was successful as all the major parts were easily identificable on the displayed heat.

Comments

An effort should be made to try to source the hearts with the major blood vessels still attached. These would provide excellent indicators for the back and the front view of the heart and also provide a better specimen of the heart with many more features to be observed.

The wall of the left ventricle is thicker than that of the right ventricle. The reason for this is that the left ventricle pump blood to all parts of the body except the lungs. The right ventricle only pumps blood to the lungs, so these walls do not need to be as thick and strong.

Possible Errors

Inaccurate cutting may make identification of structures of the heart more difficult. It is important to use your knowledge of the structure of the heart and still identify all of the important structures.

Application

Dissection of organs has long provided scientists with important information about the form and function of these organs. Dissection is important in surgery and in assessing the cause of death in autopsies.

Past Exam Questions

2004 Higher Level

Q9   (a)   (i)   Cardiac muscle may be described as a <u>contractile</u> tissue. Explain the meaning of the underlined term.
The word 'contractile' means it has the ability to contract or shorten.

(ii)   Which chamber of the heart has the greatest amount of muscle in its wall?
The left ventricle.

(b)   Describe how you dissected a mammalian heart in order to investigate the internal structure of atria and ventricles.
See the procedure on pages 116–17.

Draw a labelled diagram of your dissection to show the location and structure of the bicuspid and tricuspid valves.
See the diagram on page 119.

State the procedure that you followed to expose a semilunar valve.
To expose the semilunar valve, you cut open the aorta or the pulmonary artery and observe the valve through this cut at the base of the artery.

What is the function of a semilunar valve?
The function of the semilunar valve is to prevent the backflow of blood from an artery leaving the heart back into one of the ventricles.

Where in your dissection did you find the origin of the coronary artery?
The coronary artery originates just above the beginning of the aorta.

2006 Ordinary Level

Q7   (a)   (i)   Name the chamber of the heart that receives blood back from the lungs.
The left atrium receives blood back from the lungs.

(ii)   Name the blood vessels that bring this blood back from the lungs.
The pulmonary veins carry the blood from the lungs to the heart.

(b)   Answer the following in relation to the dissection of a heart.

(i)   What instrument did you use for the dissection?
A scalpel was used for this dissection.

(ii)   Describe how you carried out the dissection.
See the procedure on pages 116–17.

(iii)   Draw a diagram of the dissected heart and on it, label the following: bicuspid valve, left ventricle, right atrium, tricuspid valve.
See the diagram on p. 119.

Questions

1. How could the front of the heart be distinguished from the back of the heart?
2. What is the name of the blood vessels that supply the walls of the heart with oxygen and nutrients?
3. Where was the bicuspid valve located?
4. What is the name given to the chamber of the heart into which the blood enters?
5. What is the name of the artery that carries blood to the lungs?
6. What are the names of the veins that carry blood back to the heart from all the body except the lungs?
7. Why does the left side of the heart have a thicker ventricle wall?
8. What is the function of the septum?
9. Give a safety precaution that should be followed when completing this experiment.
10. Draw a diagram of the heart before dissection.

TITLE 19a Investigate the effect of exercise on the breathing rate of a human

Aim

To perform vigorous exercise and measure the effect that this had on the resting breathing rate. To be able to monitor the difference, the number of breaths will have to be taken a number of times when the person is completely at rest. The subject will then have to complete some gentle exercise and then vigorous exercise and the breathing rate will again have to be monitored continuously for a few minutes after each session of exercise. By comparing the different sets of results, the effect that exercise has on the breathing rate of a human should be clear.

Equipment and Materials

Notepad • pen • timer • volunteer.

Safety Precautions

Before beginning this experiment, ensure that you have read the procedure thoroughly and have a clear understanding of how to perform the experiment in a safe manner.

It is important that exercise (especially the vigorous exercise) is not carried out by anyone who has been sick recently, is feeling unwell or light headed or has bad asthma. If someone begins to feel unwell while carrying out this experiment, they should stop exercising immediately and rest. Medical attention should be sought if the person continues to feel unwell.

Procedure

1. Work in pairs, one person doing the exercise and the other person taking and recording results. Note that one breath consists of an inhalation and an exhalation.
2. Ensure that the person doing exercise is in a relaxed and resting state for at least five minutes before starting this experiment.
3. When at rest, the resting breathing rate is taken. Do this by counting the number of breaths taken in a minute.
4. Repeat step 3, taking the breathing rate twice more, and get the average.
5. Exercise gently for five minutes by going for a brisk walk.
6. Immediately after the gentle exercise, measure and record the breathing rate for five consecutive minutes or until the breathing rate returns to the resting rate.
7. Exercise vigorously for five minutes by running.
8. Immediately after the vigorous exercise, measure and record the breathing rate for five consecutive minutes or until the breathing rate returns to the resting rate.
9. Compare the breathing rates at rest, after gentle exercise and after vigorous exercise.

Results and Observations

Resting Breathing Rate					
	1st Minute	**2nd Minute**	**3rd Minute**	**Total**	**Average**
Person 1	11	12	10	33	11
Person 2	13	12	14	39	13

Breathing Rate after 5 Minutes of Gentle Exercise					
	1st Minute after Exercise	**2nd Minute after Exercise**	**3rd Minute after Exercise**	**4th Minute after Exercise**	**5th Minute after Exercise**
Person 1	13	12	10	11	10
Person 2	15	15	14	12	12

Breathing Rate after 5 Minutes of Vigorous Exercise					
	1st Minute after Exercise	**2nd Minute after Exercise**	**3rd Minute after Exercise**	**4th Minute after Exercise**	**5th Minute after Exercise**
Person 1	20	14	11	10	11
Person 2	23	20	15	10	11

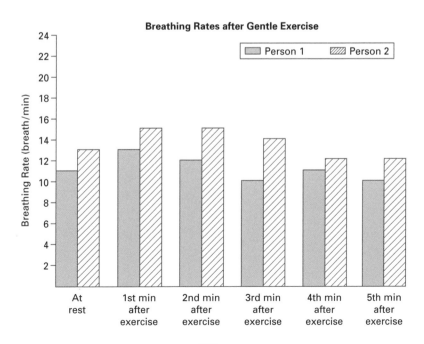

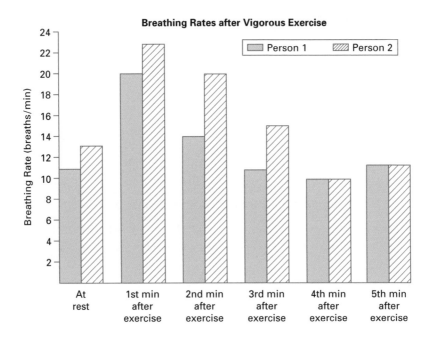

Breathing Rates after Vigorous Exercise

Control

The control for this experiment is the average resting breathing rate.

Conclusions

A person's breathing rate increases with an increased rate of exercise.

Comments

The reason for this increase in the breathing rate is that with increased activity of the body, more respiration has been taking place. This increase in respiration leads to more CO_2 being released from cells into the blood plasma. As the blood carrying this CO_2 passes through the medulla oblongata of the brain, the high CO_2 levels are measured and a series of events are triggered that results in the person excreting the high levels of CO_2 from the blood in the pulmonary artery out from the lungs into the atmosphere. At the same time, O_2 is taken in via the lungs and will be used to help fuel further aerobic respiration. As the level of exercise is decreasing, so is the level of CO_2 in the blood and as a result so is the number of breaths that need to be taken.

The normal average resting breathing rate for an adult ranges between twelve and twenty breaths per minute.

The fitter the individual, the faster their breathing rate will return to the resting rate after exercise. This is because fit people have a higher lung capacity than less fit people. For each breath the fitter person takes, a higher volume of O_2 goes into their body and releases a higher volume of CO_2 out. Therefore, the fitter person can take fewer breaths but still take in enough O_2 to provide their muscles with O_2 and to remove the CO_2 from their bodies.

Some people's breathing rate may fall below the resting rate after exercise, as the person is now taking deeper breaths. The amount of CO_2 they are excreting is the same in seventeen shallow breaths as thirteen deep breaths, for example. This also explains why fitter people tend to have a lower resting breathing rate compared to unfit people.

Possible Errors

If the person is not fully at rest when their breathing rate is being taken a false resting rate will result.

The person whose breathing rate is being measured may try to consciously alter their breathing rate, e.g. try to slow their breathing rate down on purpose. This can be easily done, as breathing can be under voluntary control. To avoid such a problem, the person whose breathing rate is being measured should try to distract themselves from their breathing.

Application

A measure of a person's fitness is an important measure of their general health. The fitter a person is, the stronger their heart and lungs will be and the more efficient their intake and distribution of oxygen and their collection and removal of CO_2 from the body. Measures of a person's fitness may also have an impact on their occupation. For example, fire fighters are required to do daily exercise to ensure they will have the strength to perform under physically stressful situations.

Past Exam Questions

2004 Ordinary Level

Q9　(a)　Answer the following in relation to human breathing rate or pulse rate.

　　　(i)　State which of these you will refer to.
　　　　　Breathing rate.

　　　(ii)　What is the average rate at rest?
　　　　　Seventeen breaths per minute.

　　　(iii)　State a possible effect of smoking on the resting rate.
　　　　　Smoking could possibly cause the resting breathing rate to increase.

　　(b)　How did you measure the resting rate?
　　　　The resting breathing rate was measured by allowing the subject to remain inactive for approximately five minutes. When they are in a fully resting state, the number of breaths they were taking per minute was counted. One breath included inhalation and expiration. This was repeated at least three times and an average was calculated and recorded.

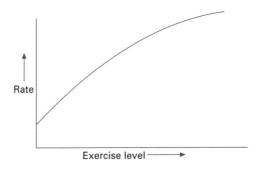

(i) Describe how you investigated the effect of exercise on this rate.
See the procedure for this experiment on p. 122.

(ii) Using the axes, draw a graph to show how rate is likely to vary as the exercise level increases.

Questions

1. Explain what exactly is meant by one breath.
2. How is external respiration (breathing) linked to internal (aerobic) respiration?
3. What is the average number of breaths per minute for an adult at rest?
4. Give a safety precaution that must be followed when carrying out this experiment.
5. Give a possible error that may occur in this experiment.
6. For the possible error mentioned in the above question, give a way in which it may be avoided.
7. Explain what conclusions can be drawn from the effect of exercise on the breathing rate.
8. Based on your results, give two ways you can identify a fit person from a less fit person from this experiment.
9. In this experiment, why might somebody's breathing rate drop below their resting breathing rate after exercise?
10. Name the part of the brain that is constantly monitoring the rate of respiration in the body and regulating our breathing rate accordingly.

TITLE 19b Investigate the effect of exercise on the pulse rate of a human

Aim

To perform vigorous exercise and measure the effect that this had on the resting pulse rate. To be able to monitor the difference, the pulse will have to be taken a number of times when the person is completely at rest. The subject will then have to complete some gentle exercise and then vigorous exercise and the pulse will again have to be monitored continuously for a few minutes after each session of exercise. By comparing the different sets of results, the effect that exercise has on the pulse of a human should be clear.

Equipment and Materials

Notepad • pen • pulse monitor (optional) • timer • volunteer.

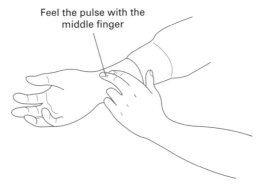

Feel the pulse with the middle finger

Safety Precautions

Before beginning this experiment, ensure that you have read the procedure thoroughly and have a clear understanding of how to perform the experiment in a safe manner.

It is important that exercise (especially the vigorous exercise) is not carried out by anyone who has been sick recently, is feeling unwell, light headed or has bad asthma. If someone begins to feel unwell while carrying out this experiment, they should stop exercising immediately and rest. Medical attention should be sought if the person continues to feel unwell.

Procedure

1. Work in pairs, one person doing the exercise and the other person taking and recording results.
2. Ensure that the person doing exercise is in a relaxed and resting state for at least five minutes before starting this experiment.
3. When at rest, the resting pulse rate is taken. Do this by counting the number of pulses felt in a minute. The pulse may be felt at the wrist or on the neck.
4. Repeat step 3, taking the pulse rate twice more, and get the average.

5. Exercise gently for five minutes by going for a brisk walk.
6. Immediately after the gentle exercise, measure and record the pulse rate every ten seconds (multiply your result by six to get the beats per minute) until the pulse rate returns to the resting rate.
7. Exercise vigorously for five minutes by running/jogging on the spot or skipping.
8. Immediately after the vigorous exercise, measure and record the pulse rate every ten seconds (multiply your result by six to get the beats per minute) until the pulse rate returns to the resting rate.
9. Compare the pulse rates at rest, after gentle exercise and after vigorous exercise.

Results and Observations

Resting Pulse Rate					
	1st Minute	2nd Minute	3rd Minute	Total	Average
Person 1	60	61	59	180	60
Person 2	75	78	78	231	77

Pulse Rate after Gentle Exercise					
	1st Minute after Exercise	2nd Minute after Exercise	3rd Minute after Exercise	4th Minute after Exercise	5th Minute after Exercise
Person 1	69	62	60	61	59
Person 2	85	80	76	77	76

Pulse Rate after Vigorous Exercise					
	1st Minute after Exercise	2nd Minute after Exercise	3rd Minute after Exercise	4th Minute after Exercise	5th Minute after Exercise
Person 1	80	72	62	60	61
Person 2	124	107	97	88	79

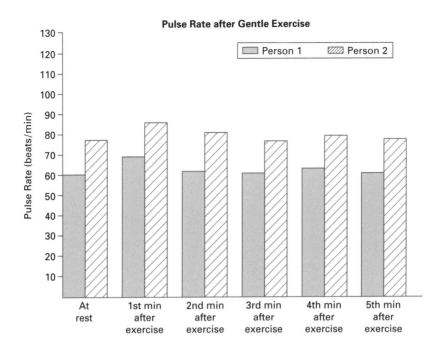

Pulse Rate after Gentle Exercise

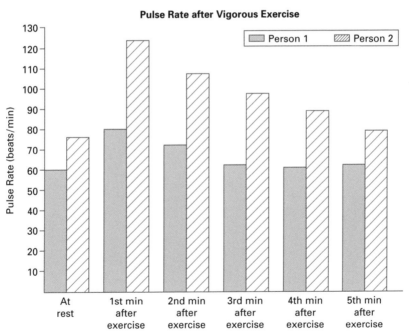

Pulse Rate after Vigorous Exercise

Control

The control for this experiment is the average resting pulse rate.

Conclusions

A person's pulse rate increases with an increased rate of exercise.

Comments

The average resting pulse rate for an adult ranges between sixty and ninety beats per minute, with seventy-two beats per minute being the most common. A person's maximum pulse rate is found using the equation 220 – age. As well as exercise, there are other factors that will affect a person's pulse rate, such as the person's age or gender.

The reasons for this increase in the pulse rate with increased activity of the body are as follows.

- The blood has to be pumped around the body faster to help to remove the increased amount of CO_2 that is being made in respiration as well as to fuel this increased amount of respiration with a greater supply of O_2.
- With increased flow of blood to the heart, the walls of the heart are stretched more. This greater stretching of the heart wall causes the heart to increase its rate of beating to remove the larger volumes of blood from the heart more quickly.

The fitter the individual, the faster their pulse rate will return to the resting rate after exercise. Fitter people have a quicker heart recovery time because the fitter person has a stronger heart muscle, which can pump more blood from the heart per beat. Therefore, the body can deliver more O_2 to the muscles and carry more CO_2 from the cells of the body to the lungs. This also explains why the pulse of a fit person tends to be lower than that of an unfit person.

The pulse rate can be measured anywhere on the body where the arteries can be found closest to the skin. Other good locations where the student may locate the pulse are the neck, temples, inner elbow and back of the knee.

Possible Errors

The person may not be fully at rest when their pulse rate is being taken, resulting in a falsely elevated resting pulse rate. As the thumb has its own pulse, if it used to count the pulse in the wrist, the two pulse rates may be measured/counted and an incorrect pulse rate will result. If the person taking the pulse presses too hard over the arteries, they may block the pulse of blood and therefore the pulse will not be felt.

Application

A measure of a person's fitness is an important measure of their general health. The more fit a person is, the stronger their heart and lungs will be and the more efficient their intake and distribution of oxygen and their collection and removal of CO_2 from the body. Measures of a person's fitness may also have an impact on their occupation. For example, fire fighters are required to do daily exercise to ensure they will have the strength to perform under physically stressful situations.

Past Exam Questions

2004 Ordinary Level

Q9　(a)　Answer the following in relation to human breathing rate or pulse rate.

State which of these you will refer to.
Pulse rate.

What is the average rate at rest?
Seventy-two beats per minute.

State a possible effect of smoking on the resting rate.
Smoking could possibly cause the resting pulse rate to rise.

(b) How did you measure the resting rate?
The resting pulse rate was measured by allowing the subject to remain
inactive for approximately five minutes. When they are in a fully resting state,
a finger was placed on their wrist where their pulse could be felt. The pulse
was counted for one minute, this was repeated at least three times and an
average was calculated and recorded. A pulse monitor could also be used.

Describe how you investigated the effect of exercise on this rate.
See the procedure for this experiment on pages 127–28.

Using the axes below, draw a graph to show how rate is likely to vary as the
exercise level increases.

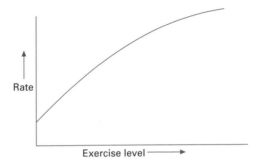

Questions

1. What is the normal average resting pulse rate of an adult?
2. Where are the best areas on the body to locate a pulse?
3. Explain the correct procedure for taking a person's pulse.
4. Why should a person not press down too firmly on the skin when taking another
   person's pulse?
5. Is a pulse taken from the vein, artery or both?
6. Give two ways in which the results of a fitter individual differ from the results that
   a less fit person would get after doing this experiment.
7. Give a safety precaution that should be adhered to when carrying out this
   experiment.
8. Give a possible error that could occur in this experiment.
9. What conclusions can be drawn from this experiment?
10. Draw a bar chart of the results that you obtained from doing this experiment.

20 Investigate the effect of IAA growth regulator on plant tissue

Aim

IAA (Indoleacetic Acid) is a plant growth regulator that has different effects on the roots and shoots of a plant at different concentrations. The aim of this experiment is to observe the different rates of growth in the root and the shoots of a plant when these areas are exposed to different concentrations of this growth regulator.

Equipment and Materials

Acetate sheet • adhesive tape • cotton wool (absorbent) • distilled water • ethanol • filter paper • graduated cylinder • graph paper • IAA • Petri dishes • pipettes • radish seeds • test tubes • test tube rack • thermometer.

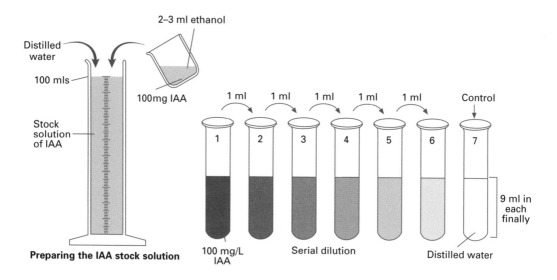

Preparing the IAA stock solution

Serial dilution

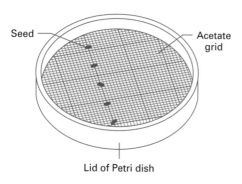

Position the seeds on the grid in Petri dish lid

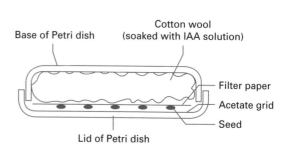

Seed exposed to an IAA solution

Safety Precautions

Before beginning this experiment, ensure that you have read the procedure thoroughly and have a clear understanding of how to perform the experiment in a safe manner.

Ethanol is highly flammable and therefore needs to be used away from sources of heat and in a well-ventilated area. Irritation is caused if it comes in contact with the eyes, so safety glasses must be worn.

Highly
Flammable

Harmful

IAA may cause irritation to the skin, eyes or respiratory system on contact. Safety glasses should be worn and the laboratory should be adequately ventilated.

Procedure

1. Dissolve 100 mg of IAA into 3 ml of ethanol (IAA dissolves better in ethanol than it does in distilled water).
2. Once the IAA has dissolved, bring it up to 1 litre using distilled water. This solution now has a concentration of 100 mg/L.
3. Perform a serial dilution. Start by labelling seven test tubes 1 to 7.
4. In the first test tube, using a clean pipette, place 10 ml of the 100 mg/L solution.
5. Using a clean pipette, place 9 ml of distilled water in the remaining six test tubes (2 to 7).
6. Using a clean pipette, place 1 ml of the solution from test tube 1 into test tube 2. Using a clean glass rod, stir the solution in test tube 2 completely to ensure an even concentration of IAA throughout.
7. Repeat step 6 by putting 1 ml from test tube 2 into 3, from test tube 3 into 4, from test tube 4 into 5 and from test tube 5 to 6.
8. Test tube 7 has only the distilled water put into it, as it is the control for this experiment.
9. The concentrations of IAA in the different solutions in each test tube are as follows.

Test Tube	1	2	3	4	5	6	7
IAA Concentration (mg/L)	100	10	1	0.1	0.01	0.001	0

10. Now take seven Petri dishes and label them 1 to 7.
11. In each lid of the Petri dishes, place a disc of acetate on which graph paper has been photocopied. (This will enable a more accurate measurement of root and shoot growth to be taken.)
12. Place four seeds onto the acetate in each of the Petri dishes.

13. Place a circle of filter paper (the same diameter of the Petri dish) onto the seeds in each Petri dish.
14. Place a few drops of the solution from the Petri dish's corresponding test tube onto the filter paper over the seeds.
15. Cover all the filter paper with a thick layer of cotton wool.
16. Pour the remaining solution from each of the test tubes onto the cotton wool of its corresponding Petri dish. The cotton wool and filter paper will keep the solutions in contact with the seeds for the duration of the experiment.
17. Seal the Petri dishes and ensure that they are labelled with the concentration of IAA that is on the seeds of that Petri dish.
18. Stand all of the Petri dishes on their edges so that the roots and shoots have the maximum available space to grow. The Petri dishes will need to be supported, by books, for example, to prevent them from rolling.
19. Place the Petri dishes in an incubator at 25°C for two to three days.
20. After two or three days, remove the Petri dishes and measure the amount of growth that has occurred with the roots and the shoots.

Results and Observations

Give a list of growth measurements at the different concentrations of IAA.

Length of Roots (mm)						
IAA Concentration	Seed 1	Seed 2	Seed 3	Seed 4	Average	% Stimulation or Inhibition
10^2 ppm	0	0	0	0	0	−100
10 ppm	0.1	0	0	0.1	0.05	−98
1 ppm	0.4	0.4	0.5	0.3	0.4	−80
10^{-1} ppm	1.5	1.5	1.3	1.3	1.4	−30
10^{-2} ppm	1.8	2	2	1.8	1.9	−5
10^{-3} ppm	2.3	2.4	2.2	2.4	2.4	20
Water (Control)	1.5	2.5	2	2	2	

Length of Shoots (mm)						
IAA Concentration	Seed 1	Seed 2	Seed 3	Seed 4	Average	% Stimulation or Inhibition
10^2 ppm	3.5	3.5	3.5	3.5	3.5	75
10 ppm	6	5	6	6.5	6	200
1 ppm	5	5	4	6	5	150
10^{-1} ppm	3.5	3.5	3.7	3.7	3.6	80
10^{-2} ppm	2.2	2.2	2.2	2.3	2.2	10
10^{-3} ppm	2	1.75	2	2.2	2	0
Water (Control)	2	2	2	2.1	2	

$$\% \text{ stimulation or inhibition} = \frac{\text{average length} - \text{average length of control}}{\text{average length of control}} \times \frac{100}{1}$$

Formula to calculate the percentage stimulation or inhibition of root or shoot growth related to concentration of IAA.

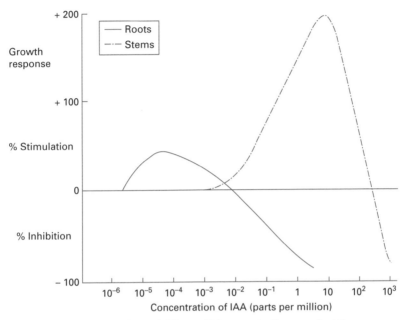

Effects of different IAA concentrations on plant tissues

Control

The control of this experiment is the seeds where no IAA, i.e. just water, was added.

Conclusions

The roots grow more vigorously at lower concentrations of IAA, whereas the shoots grow more vigorously at higher concentrations of IAA.

Possible Errors

The step where most errors are likely to occur is when carrying out the serial dilution. It is important that each step of the serial dilution is carried out using clean pipettes. Also, each time a solution is added to a Petri dish, the solution needs to be mixed thoroughly to ensure that the concentration of IAA is evenly distributed throughout the Petri dish. If these precautions are not adhered to, the final concentrations of the solutions in the serial dilution may be incorrect.

It is important that the Petri dishes are stood on their edges so that the roots and shoots will have enough space in which to grow.

IAA is a plant regulator that is often used in the production of rooting powders. Rooting powders are mainly used in the gardening industry to help stimulate the growth of roots from cuttings of plants. Knowledge of the concentration of IAA that best stimulates the growth of roots is important in the production of these artificial growth stimulators.

Past Exam Questions

2006 Higher Level

Q7 (b) In the case of each of the following state:

    1. An investigation in which you used it.

    2. The precise purpose for its use in the investigation that you have indicated.

    (i) *IAA*.

    1. To investigate the effect of IAA growth regulator on plant tissue.

    2. Different concentrated solutions of IAA were placed on seeds to determine IAA's stimulatory or inhibitory effect on root and shoot growth.

Questions

1. What does IAA stand for?
2. What is meant by a serial dilution?
3. Why was more than one seed placed in each Petri dish?
4. What was the control that was used in this experiment?
5. Why were the Petri dishes placed on their edges?
6. What temperature were these Petri dishes placed at?
7. What were the results that were seen in the roots at the different concentrations of IAA?
8. What were the results that were seen in the shoots at the different concentrations of IAA?
9. Give a safety precaution that should be followed when performing this experiment.
10. Give an application of this experiment.

21 Investigate the effect of water, oxygen and adequate temperature on germination

Aim

To determine the effect that water, oxygen and adequate temperature have on the germination of seeds. To investigate this, a large sample of seeds will be given all of the above variables and three other groups of seeds will each be missing one factor. The resulting effect on germination will be noted.

Equipment and Materials

Cotton wool (absorbent) • anaerobic jar • distilled water • fridge • incubator • labels • lamp/torch • oil • Petri dishes • radish seeds • test tube holder (tongs) • test tube racks • test tubes • water bath • waterproof pen.

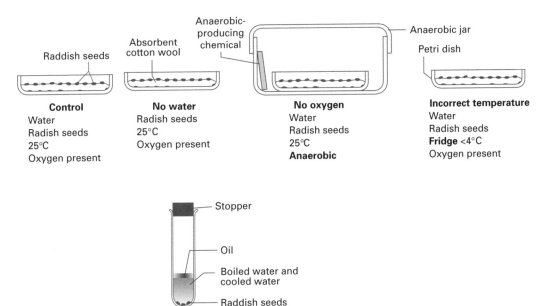

Safety Precautions

Before beginning this experiment, ensure that you have read the procedure thoroughly and have a clear understanding of how to perform the experiment in a safe manner.

Caution should be exercised when using the water bath, as steam and splashes from the boiling water can cause severe burns.

Procedure

1. Turn on the water bath and set to 100°C. Allow it to reach this temperature while carrying out the rest of the experiment.
2. Label Petri dishes as 'Control', 'No Water', 'No Oxygen' and 'Incorrect Temperature'.
3. Cover the base of each of the Petri dishes with the absorbent cotton wool.

4. Add ten radish seeds onto the cotton wool of each of the Petri dishes.

Petri Dish A: 'Control'

1. The 'Control' Petri dish requires all three variables to be present in ample amounts for three to four days.
2. Provide water by moistening the cotton wool in this Petri dish by adding 10 ml of water. Over the following days, note whether the cotton wool is drying out. If so, moisten it by adding more water, as required.
3. Provide oxygen by allowing the seeds to be in contact with free air.
4. Provide adequate temperature for the seeds by placing the seeds at room temperature or by placing them in an incubator set to 25°C.

Petri Dish B: 'No Water'

1. This Petri dish is to receive ample amounts of oxygen and adequate temperature but no water for three to four days.
2. Do not add any water to the cotton wool, thereby removing moisture.
3. Provide oxygen by allowing the seeds to be in contact with free air.
4. Provide adequate temperature for the seeds by placing the seeds at room temperature or by placing them in an incubator set to 25°C.

Petri Dish C: 'No Oxygen'

1. This Petri dish is to receive ample amounts of water and adequate temperature but no oxygen for three to four days.
2. Provide water by moistening the cotton wool in this Petri dish by adding 10 ml of water. Over the following days, note whether the cotton wool is drying out. If so, moisten it by adding more water, as required.
3. Do not provide any oxygen. Anaerobic conditions can be achieved by using an anaerobic jar (containing alkaline pyrogallol), as per its instructions. Alternatively, if there is no access to anaerobic jars, oxygen can be eliminated by boiling some distilled water in a boiling tube in the water bath. Once the water has boiled, remove the boiling tube using a set of tongs and place in a test tube rack. Leave the water in the test tube to cool. Once the water has completely cooled, the ten radish seeds can be dropped into the water. Add a 1 cm layer of oil over the water by carefully pouring the oil down the side of the test tube.
4. Provide adequate temperature for the seeds by placing the seeds at room temperature or by placing them in an incubator set to 25°C.

Petri Dish D: 'Incorrect Temperature'

1. This Petri dish is to receive ample amounts of water and oxygen but not an adequate temperature for three to four days.
2. Provide water by moistening the cotton wool in this Petri dish by adding 10 ml of water. Over the following days, note whether the cotton wool is drying out. If so, moisten it by adding more water, as required.
3. Provide oxygen by allowing the seeds to be in contact with free air.
4. Provide inadequate temperature for the seeds by placing the seeds in a refrigerator (less than 4°C). As these are small seeds and many small seeds require light to

germinate, we will ensure there is light in the refrigerator by shining a lit torch onto the Petri dish while in the refrigerator during school hours.

Obtaining Results

1. After three to four days have elapsed, place all four Petri dishes on the bench and observe if germination has occurred in any of them. Record your results.

Results and Observations

Germination only occurred in the control Petri dish. The other Petri dishes appear the same as they had at the start of the experiment three or four days previously.

Test Tube	Variables Present	Variable Absent	Germination (Yes/No)
A	Water, oxygen, adequate temperature	None	Yes
B	Oxygen, adequate temperature	Water	No
C	Water, adequate temperature	Oxygen	No
D	Water, oxygen	Adequate temperature	No

Control

The control in this experiment was the Petri dish that contained all the correct levels of all the variables (water, oxygen and an adequate temperature).

Conclusions

Water, oxygen and an adequate temperature have to be present in the environment of the seed if germination is to occur.

Comments

From the results of this experiment, it is clear that all three of the factors being investigated have to be present if germination is to occur.

The water is required, as all metabolic reactions occur in an aqueous environment, which allows the enzymes to move and come in contact with their substrate. Water is also used in some reactions, e.g. hydrolysis, which is responsible for the digestion of the seed's food store. The water may also help to soften the embryo of the seed and therefore allow the radicle and plumule to emerge.

The oxygen is required so that aerobic respiration can occur in the seed, therefore releasing the maximum amount of energy and enabling the embryo (especially the radicle and plumule) to grow.

An adequate temperature is required so that the enzymes in the seed will work at their optimum rate. This will result in the reactions occurring at their optimum rate and the embryo growing at its maximum rate. If the temperature is too low, the embryo will fail to grow and therefore germination will not occur.

Possible Errors

One of the principles of good experimentation is to try to have a large sample size, as this will prevent results that are due to individual variables. In this experiment, we provide a large sample size by placing ten seeds in each test tube instead of just one seed. If we used just one seed, it might have been a damaged seed and may never have germinated no matter how much water, oxygen and temperature we gave it. By using ten seeds, there is less of a chance of this happening, as there is less of a chance that all ten seeds are damaged and therefore we are more likely to get accurate results in our experiment.

Another step where an error may occur is when the seeds are dropped into water which has been boiled. If the seeds are added to the water before it has had a chance to cool, the high temperatures may denature the enzymes in the seeds that are necessary for germination to occur, and, as a result, germination would never occur even if all the necessary conditions are met. Therefore, the water must be allowed to cool so that the seeds' enzymes are not denatured and we can be sure that the lack of germination was as a result of a lack of oxygen and not as a result of denatured enzymes.

Application

The knowledge of what factors are needed for germination to occur is important in horticulture (gardening) and agriculture (farming). With the knowledge that water, oxygen and adequate temperature are needed for all seeds to germinate, germination can be induced whenever required. There are other factors that are required for germination to occur in certain seeds. For example, small seeds, e.g. grass seeds, tend to also require light, as they only have a small food store and need to be near the surface of the soil so that they will be able to begin photosynthesis almost immediately. Large seeds often also require darkness before they will germinate; they have a large food store so they need darkness deep in the soil, where they will be able to strongly anchor the plant and be close to water and nutrient supplies.

Past Exam Questions

2006 Higher Level

Q7   (b)   In the case of each of the following state:

1.   An investigation in which you used it.

2.   The precise purpose for its use in the investigation that you have indicated.

(iv)   *Alkaline pyrogallol or anaerobic jar.*

1.   To investigate the effect of water, oxygen and adequate temperature on germination.

2.   This is used to remove the oxygen from the presence of some seeds being used in this experiment.

2005 Ordinary Level

Q9 (a) (i) What is meant by the germination of a seed?
Germination is the growth of the embryo plant from the seed.

(ii) State one reason why water is needed for germination.
An aqueous environment is required if any metabolic reaction is to occur. Therefore, water is needed for the enzymes to become mobilised so that they can digest the food stored in the seed. Water also has a role to play in the digestion (hydrolysis) of the food store.

(b) Answer the following questions in relation to an experiment that you carried out to investigate the effects of water, oxygen and temperature on germination.

(i) Draw a labelled diagram of the apparatus that you used.
See the diagram on p. 137.

(ii) Describe how you carried out the experiment.
See the procedure on pages 137–39.

(iii) Describe the results of this experiment, including the result of the control.
See Results and Observations on page 139.

Questions

1. Why does a seed require water to germinate?
2. Why does a seed require oxygen to germinate?
3. Why does a seed require an adequate temperature to germinate?
4. Why were ten seeds used in each test tube instead of just one?
5. How were each of the factors varied?
6. What was the control in this experiment?
7. Why might a torch be used as a light source when the Petri dish containing the seeds is placed into the refrigerator?
8. Give a safety precaution that you would exercise when carrying out this experiment.
9. Give a possible error that may occur while carrying out this experiment.
10. Suggest an application of this experiment.

Aim

To show that seeds have enzymes that are capable of digestion. We will use starch agar plates to place the seeds on. The starch will be the substrate that the enzymes will digest. The presence of starch can be measured by the iodine.

Equipment and Materials

Alcohol • beakers • Bunsen burner • chopping board • cotton wool • disinfectant • disposable gloves • distilled water • dropper • ethanol • forceps • incubator • iodine • labels • large seeds, e.g. broad beans • masking tape • matches • nutrient starch agar plates • paper towels • Petri dishes • scalpels • shallow dish, e.g. clock dish • thermometer • timer • water bath • waterproof pen.

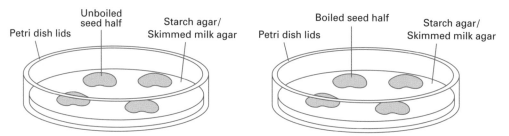

Seeds positioned in Petri dishes to demonstrate digestive activity during germination

Safety Precautions

Before beginning this experiment, ensure that you have read the procedure thoroughly and have a clear understanding of how to perform the experiment in a safe manner.

Caution should be exercised when using the water bath, as steam and splashes from the boiling water can cause severe burns.

Iodine is harmful if swallowed, inhaled or if it comes in contact with the skin or eyes. A lab coat, disposable gloves and protective safety glasses should be worn while performing this experiment. Iodine should only be used in a well-ventilated area.

Toxic

Corrosive

Caution should be exercised when using sharp blades. The cutting should always be done on a chopping board and the direction of the cutting should be away from the person's body.

Ethanol is highly flammable and therefore needs to be used away from sources of heat and in a well-ventilated area. Irritation is caused if it comes in contact with the eyes, so safety glasses must be worn.

Highly
Flammable

Harmful

Procedure

1. Soak the seeds in distilled water for one to two days.
2. Allow the seeds to begin germinating by placing them in Petri dishes containing absorbent, moist cotton wool. These Petri dishes also require the correct temperature and oxygen.
3. When they have begun to germinate, use a flamed scalpel to split all the beans lengthwise on a sterilised chopping board.
4. Divide the cut broad bean seeds into two groups, one group to show digestion by the seeds and one to act as the control.
5. Place the control beans into a beaker of water and then place the beaker carefully into the water bath. Turn on the water bath and set to boiling (100°C).
6. When the seeds have been boiled, let the water cool. Using a flamed forceps, remove the seeds from the beaker.
7. Fill a shallow dish with alcohol. Using the flamed forceps, pick up a boiled cut bean and wash it in the alcohol. Using the other hand, remove the lid off a Petri dish and quickly place the bean cut side down onto the agar. Repeat this step until all four half-beans are face down on the agar. (The beans are placed face down so that the enzymes will have direct contact with the agar.)
8. Seal this Petri dish with the tape, label the underside of the Petri dish as 'Boiled Beans' and place it in an incubator at 25°C for two days.
9. Repeat steps 7 and 8, but this time with the unboiled cut beans.
10. After two days, remove the boiled cut bean Petri dish from the incubator and unseal the dish. Using a forceps, remove the beans from the surface of the agar.
11. Using a dropper, place iodine all over the surface of the agar and allow to soak for five minutes. After five minutes, pour off any excess iodine and observe the colour of the agar.
12. Repeat steps 10 and 11 using the unboiled cut beans.

Results and Observations

In the Petri dish that contained the unboiled cut beans, the agar surrounding where the beans had been located stained red-yellow and the rest of the agar stained blue-black.

In the dish that contained the boiled cut beans, all the agar stained blue-black.

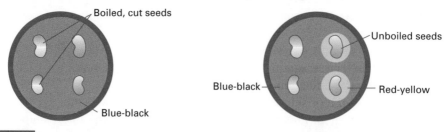

Control

The control for this experiment is the Petri dish that contained the boiled cut beans.

Conclusions

The agar stained red-yellow in the Petri dish that contained the unboiled cut seeds, as the amylase enzymes in the seeds had digested the starch to maltose.

In the Petri dish that contained the boiled cut seeds, all the agar stained blue-black, as by boiling the seeds we had denatured the amylase enzymes and the enzyme was no longer able to work. Thus the starch was not digested and all the agar stained blue-black.

Comments

It is important to soak the seeds in water for at least twenty-four hours prior to use in the experiment. This will ensure that any enzyme inhibitor in the seeds will have been given enough of an opportunity to be broken down. Once the inhibitors have been broken down, the digestive enzymes used in germination will be activated.

Possible Errors

Aseptic techniques may not be observed during this experiment. If micro-organisms get onto the agar, they may be the cause of digestion of the starch rather than the enzymes in the seeds. Examples of the aseptic techniques required are flaming the scalpel and forceps. Also, the lids of the nutrient agar plates need to be closed swiftly in order to prevent the experiment from becoming contaminated with micro-organisms. The consequence of this is that a false positive may result as we my attribute the digestion of the agar to the beans even though it could have been caused by micro-organisms.

Ensure that the beans are face down on the agar. If they are placed the other way, the testa will block the enzymes from having contact with the starch and therefore no digestion will take place.

Application

The information on digestive enzymes in germinating seeds is of great importance to the horticulture and agriculture industries.

Past Exam Questions

2006 Higher Level

Q7   (b)   In the case of each of the following state:

144

1. An investigation in which you used it.

2. The precise purpose for its use in the investigation that you have indicated.

(ii) *Starch agar or skimmed milk plates*.

1. To use starch agar of skimmed milk plates to show digestive activity during germination.

2. The starch or skimmed milk plates provided the substrate for enzymes present in germinating seeds. The breakdown of the starch in the agar showed the digestive properties of the enzymes in the germinating seeds.

2006 Ordinary Level

Q9 (a) (i) Give one location in a seed in which food is stored.
Food can be found in the endosperm or cotyledon.

(ii) Name a carbohydrate that you would expect to be present in this food store.
Starch.

(b) In your practical work, you investigated digestive activity during germination.

(i) What type of agar did you use in this investigation?
Starch agar or skimmed milk agar.

(ii) Describe how you carried out the investigation. Refer to a control in your answer.
See the procedure on page 143.

(iii) Describe the results of your investigation.
The results show that when iodine is added to the agar with the unboiled seeds, the agar remained a red-orange colour, as there was no starch. When the iodine was added to the agar plate with the boiled seeds, the starch turned blue-black, as the seeds were unable to digest the starch.

Questions

1. What types of seeds were used for this experiment?
2. Name the food source that is in the agar and name what enzyme can digest this food source.
3. Why was more than one half seed used in each agar plate?
4. Why were some of the seeds boiled?
5. At what temperature should these seeds be placed in the incubator?
6. How will the results of this experiment be measured?
7. Why were aseptic techniques used in this experiment?
8. What is a safety precaution that should be followed when carrying out this experiment?
9. Draw a diagram of the results that you would expect to see with the unboiled and boiled seeds.
10. Give a possible error that could occur in this experiment.

Laboratory Rules for Pupils

1. Do not enter the laboratory without permission.
2. Do not use any equipment unless permitted to do so by the teacher. Make sure you know exactly what you are supposed to do. If in doubt, ask the teacher.
3. Long hair must always be tied back securely.
4. Always wear eye protection when instructed to do so.
5. Always check that the label on the bottle is exactly the same as the material you require. If in doubt, ask the teacher.
6. Nothing must be tasted, eaten or drunk in the laboratory.
7. Any substance accidentally taken into the mouth must be spat out immediately and the mouth washed out with plenty of water. The incident must be reported to the teacher.
8. Any cut, burn or other accident must be reported at once to the teacher.
9. Any chemicals spilled on the skin or clothing must be washed at once with plenty of water and reported to teacher.
10. Always wash your hands after practical work.

'Safety in School Science 2001', Department of Education and Science